The Top Ninja Dual Zone Air Fryer Cookbook UK

Easy and Fabulous Ninja Foodi Air Fryer Recipes You Will Love | Favorites for Side Dishes, Desserts, and Snacks, Incl.

Cheryl H. Charlton

Contents

All about the Ninja Dual Zone Air Fryer.

The Ninja air fryer has significantly changed my life, and I don't say it lightly. By including two air frying baskets in one machine, you may prepare two components of your dinner at the same time, using various cooking modes and temperatures.

To be honest, the primary issue with the greatest air fryers is that they can only accomplish one thing at a time. When you buy an air fryer, you'll want it to cook anything from your morning bacon to your pan-fried vegetables, and the Ninja Fryer Dual Zone can do both.

When testing the Ninja fryer Dual Zone, I used a combination of my recipes and those provided with the air fryer. Because air fryers cook quicker than ovens, you may need to alter cooking timings if converting from a standard oven.

The Ninja Fryer Dual Zone, on the other hand, will also create a massive impact in your life if you follow all the directives.

This is not your typical air fryer. Because of the multiple compartments, it has an extremely broad shape, so you'll need a lot of space to keep it. If you wish to keep it on display, it won't seem out of place in your upscale kitchen.

The digital screen, matte surface, and chromed accents look amazing, and despite feeling like its parts are made of plastic (and resembling a large bread bucket), it comes off as a quality product.

It's fantastic value for money when compared to other versions on the market. Any excellent air fryer can be costly, and nearly none of them come with an extra frying basket or as many functions as the Ninja.

A huge control panel in the front controls all functions. Interestingly, there are no one-touch controls, although there are lots of preset programs like roasting, baking and dehydrating.

There are two chromed handles below the panel that you may pull toward you to gain access to the air fryer's cooking baskets. Each one can carry up to 3.8 litres of ingredients, for a total of 7.6 litres.

Each chamber contains a crisper panel, which helps to brown the food while air-frying; it allows air to flow around the food, removing unnecessary moisture and ensuring a crispy, brown touch.

They also keep food from clinging to the bottom of each container. I found the panels straightforward to remove for cleaning, either manually or by using a dishwasher.

In addition to air frying, the device can max crisp, dehydrate, roast, reheat and bake, and all of these capabilities are noted on the digitally controlled screen. It has also a timer that allows you to see how much cooking time is left in each segment.

Because there is no stirring stick inside,

you will need to stir or shake the food from time to time to encourage equal browning.

Otherwise, the Ninja functions similarly to most other air fryers by circulating hot air over your food, creating a similar effect to deep frying, the difference is that you will usually just require a tablespoon or so of cooking oil.

Apart from being able to prepare food with minimal to no oil, it can cook two distinct items at the same time and guarantee they're ready to serve simultaneously.

It's a huge device in terms of how other countertop appliances are, with a measurement of H31.5 x D35cm. With its size, it's still elegant and appealing, as well as useful. With a stylish black and chrome appearance, it's the type of device that no one would mind sitting on their worktop if they have extra space.

The gadget is elegantly built and feels comfortable to handle. It has two independent cooking drawers that effortlessly pull out to give you a total capacity of 7.6 litres. Each chamber is deep enough to prepare a substantial amount of food, such as 500g of potato fries, 1kg of chicken, or up to 12 cakes. The drawer knobs are comfortable and simple to insert and remove.

Benefits of using Ninja air fryer.

What is the appeal of Ninja air fryers? Do they meet up to the standard as their promoters claim? According to my own experience evaluating numerous models and user comments, these are the top ten advantages of Ninja air fryers.

Makes crispy food

The Max Crisp feature is intended for frozen meals, particularly a small amount of frozen food such as oven chips and chicken nuggets. This option, which automatically warms up to 240 degrees, burns the breading before the interior was cooked on several bigger frozen breaded chicken fillets.

However, for smaller frozen things such as fish fingers, scampi, vegetable nuggets, frozen fries, and more, it gave a wonderfully crispy surface and was properly cooked within. It also achieved this much faster than the cooking instructions on the carton stated, allowing you to maintain an eye on your food while it cooks as you adjust to the Dual Zone.

I'd prefer using the usual air fry setting for frozen fish fillets or other bigger frozen foods, where you can modify the temperature to allow for the fact that they will take longer to cook.

A healthy meal

The result of using little or no oil leads to the cooking of excellent dishes in your air fryer. Optionally, if you decided to use small quantities of oil, the amounts used are insignificant since oil drops off the food when cooking and collects at the basket. Consequently, in the end you are going to use less amounts of oil and consume relatively fewer calories.

Also, you receive the extra benefit of avoiding the carcinogens associated with deep-dried meals, notably acrylamide. The chemical compound formed when carbohydrate-rich meals like potatoes are deep-fried and dried, is usually classified by the Agency for Cancer Research as a potential human carcinogen.

While research continues, it is anticipated that air fryers may help reduce the acrylamide levels produced by oil-based high-heat cooking.

A safe way of cooking

When compared to the traditional ways of frying food which required the use of a lot of oil, the Ninja air fryer is safer. Traditionally a lot of oil was used which could be dangerous once the heated oil explodes and goes on your skin or clothes. In air frying, less oil was used and cooking was done in an enclosed system.

To stay safe, precautions need to be taken while using this device. Your air fryer might still remain very hot. So, when opening you air fryer during cooking, wear heat-safe gloves or oven mitts.

Cons of using Ninja dual-zone air fryer.

When using Ninja dual-zone air fryer, it does not inevitably make the food nutritious. Aside from that, you are restricted in what you can prepare.

The amount of time and temperature may differ, so there will be a period of adjustment and you may waste a lot of food before you get to know how to operate it.

Below are a few challenges that you may encounter while using the air fryer.

- Cleaning a Ninja air fryer may take longer as compared to using an oven.
- It can be costly, big and difficult to store, loud, and have a restricted frying capacity.
- Ninja air fryers have been popular for some years, but they are only worthwhile if they match your lifestyle. If you have a large family, it will take too long to prepare a supper for everyone. However, it might be the ideal kitchen update for couples or anyone searching for methods to prepare fast meals with less oil.
- You might get disappointed if you had anticipated the reheat feature to behave similarly to that of a microwave. Despite its ability to revive leftovers, it is not a replacement for a normal microwave, which can prepare ready meals as well as reheat and melt beverages.

Cleaning & Maintaining

In many families, the Ninja Air Fryer is now a popular kitchen appliance. It cooks meals quickly and very simple tooperate.

Just like other kitchen equipment, you must maintain your Ninja Air Fryer clean for it to function properly and last a long time. It is critical to properly maintain the equipment to reap its maximum benefits. A filthy air fryer creates undesirable aromas and scents that might ruin your final food.

1. Turn off and disconnect the gadget.

To avoid getting electrocuted, the initial and most crucial step in cleaning this incredible gadget is to switch it off and disconnect it from the socket. Unfortunately, regardless of how basic this is supposed to be, we frequently forget to disconnect electrical equipment before thoroughly cleaning them.

Allow the fryer to cool down for a short time after use to avoid being scorched in case it is still hot and to safeguard the machine from damage.

2. Removable components are to be cleaned using a dishwasher

The simplicity with which all the replaceable elements of a Ninja Air fryer can be cleaned in your dishwasher is one of its greatest features. Remove the dishwasher-safe frying basket, crisper plate and rack first, then wash them in the same manner as other dishes.

To remove any burned-on or stuck-on food, you may also consider soaking them in soap, vinegar, and relatively hot water solution beforehand. Then, after taking the components out of the dishwasher, gently wipe out any leftover grime and properly dry all the attachments before using them once more.

3. How to clean the interior of the Ninja Air Fryer

Take a soft sponge or washcloth and moisturize it with hot water. Turn your heating elements upside-down and use the sponge to clean them. If hot water alone is insufficient to remove any stubborn oil from the heating element, add a little amount of dish soap to the water.

A quick tip: To thoroughly remove any stuck-on food on the heating elements, use food brushes with soft bristles and a dishwashing solution.

Before attempting to use your Ninja Air Fryer again, clean the inside using the same procedures and allow it to fully dry.

Exterior cleaning

Dampen a cloth or sponge in a mixture of mild detergent (ammonia, dish soap, surface cleansers, etc.) and relatively hot water. When cleaning the exterior of your air fryer, never use too much water.

4. Maintenance

To avoid a buildup of oil and food particles on the attachments and surfaces of your air fryer, clean it immediately after each use. After cleaning, properly dry the device and put it in a dry area (preferably the box it came in or cabinets where dirt and dust cannot readily reach).

To avoid overfilling or incorrectly using the

basket, ensure you follow the recommendations in the handbook. This might harm the heating element, causing your fryer to malfunction.

Tips for Using an Air Fryer

- First, preheat your Ninja air fryer - yeah, this may sound obvious, but trust me, most people will simply dump in a frozen bag of fries, fire it up, and then get upset when the fries aren't done at the 14-17 minute point. An example is when you want to cook something using your oven. The cooking will start once it has reached a specific temperature. Alternatively, when using a pressure cooker, pressure must build before beginning to pressure cook.
- Coat the tray or pan with oil - A small coating is all that is required to keep the meals from sticking.
- COOKING SPRAY SHOULD NEVER BE USED - nonstick aerosol sprays can cause harm to your air fryer. Coat your tray and meals with an oil mister.

Cooking Techniques using the Ninja Air Fryer

- Coating with Oil - Even though this is an air fryer, you will still need to add some oil to aid with the "fried" component. Lightly coat your food with oil before placing it in the basket or tray. If you have fattier meals like bacon, you do not need to bathe it with oil.
- Never overcrowd the tray or basket with more than one layer. Only certain items will crisp if you do this, while others will be mushy or not browned.
- Cook in batches - this corresponds to the single layer. Doing so guarantees that your foods are consistently browned and crisp.
- Shake it/Flip it! To guarantee consistent cooking, pull the basket out and shake it every few minutes during the cooking time. Pull out a tray, turn the meals, and continue air frying.
- Spray Halfway through - If you want something extremely "fried" crispy, gently spritz it with oil halfway through cooking. However, only do this after you have completely removed the basket or tray from the air fryer. Never add oil while the food/tray is still inside the device. Adding the oil while the machine is still running might result in a sticky buildup and sludge within.

Tricks to using Ninja air fryer

- Getting rid of smoke-When frying extremely oily meals like bacon or beef, your air fryer might emit white smoke. One shouldn't get concerned. To solve this, put roughly 2 tablespoons of water or a slice of bread in the bottom of the basket to absorb any grease. Bread not only solves the smoke problem, but it also collects grease and makes cleanup easier!
- Reheating - As most people do, you only use the microwave to make popcorn or melt butter. The same is true for reheating meals. Use the air fryer instead of the microwave. You'll receive a thousand times greater outcomes!
- Cleaning can be a pain if you have an air fryer metal tray/basket. However, I purchased these

air fryer mats, which significantly reduce cleanup time. They may also be trimmed to any size to fit the basket and are reusable.

- Hand-wash the basket or tray in hot, soapy water. Use a nylon bristol brush to assist scrape clean the nooks and crannies of a metal tray.

Frequent Q&A

- Is it necessary to use oil when air frying?

Although oil is not required, we suggest starting with 1 tablespoon and modifying to taste, or referring to the recipe for recommended oil levels.

- Can I prepare different dishes in each zone without fear of cross-contamination?

Yes, each zone is self-contained, with its heat source and fans.

- How can I tell if the device is turned on?

When you turn on the device, the digital display will read 0:00.

- How do I know when to use Max Crisp rather than Air Fry?

When preparing frozen food, like french fries or chicken nuggets, use Max Crisp for the best results. The temperature is set at 240°C and can't be altered. This high temperature is ideal for small amounts of breaded or battered foods, producing a crispy, crunchy result.

- How do I interpret the time setting?

The time is shown in HH: MM (hours, minutes).

- Why isn't the temperature rising?

This indicates that you have already reached the maximum temperature for that setting.

- Is it necessary to preheat the unit?

No. It does not need preheating.

- How can I stop one zone when I'm utilizing both?

To stop one zone, hit the zone button first, then the dial. Simply push the dial to halt both zones.

- How full can I make the drawers?

There isn't a fill line. Check that the drawer in the unit can close correctly. For optimum results, do not overfill the drawers so that hot air can circulate evenly and Ingredients can be mixed often.

- Is it necessary to thaw frozen items before air frying?

It is dependent on the meal. Follow the package directions.

Air-fryer doughnuts

Prep:30 mins / Cook:25 mins plus overnight proving / Serves 6-8

Ingredients

- 275g plain flour, plus extra for dusting
- ½ tsp ground cinnamon (optional)
- 1 egg, beaten
- For the glaze
- 125g icing sugar
- 3 tbsp milk
- ¼ tsp vanilla extract
- 125ml milk, lukewarm
- 50g unsalted butter, melted and cooled to lukewarm
- 7g sachet dried fast-action yeast
- 60g caster sugar
- 1 tsp vanilla extract
- flavourless oil, for proving

Preparation Instructions

1. In a stand mixer's bowl, combine the milk, melted butter, yeast, 1 tsp. of sugar, and vanilla essence. The yeast needs to activate for 8–10 minutes.

2. Combine the remaining sugar, flour, 1/2 tsp salt, and cinnamon, if using, in a separate basin. After incorporating the dry ingredients, stir the beaten egg into the milk mixture. Once the dough is elastic and smooth, knead it with a dough hook on medium speed for 5 to 8 minutes. You may alternatively use your hands to knead the dough for 10 to 12 minutes, or until it is smooth. Keep your patience since the dough is quite sticky.

3. Once the dough has doubled in size, transfer to a basin that has been lightly oiled, cover with a clean tea towel, and set aside in a warm location for 1 hour and 30 minutes. Roll out the dough to a thickness of about 1.5 cm on a lightly dusted board. Make your doughnuts by cutting them out using a cutter or two (1 x 7.5cm and 1 x 2.5cm for the middle). Put the doughnuts and, if desired, the doughnut centers on a prepared baking sheet, then cover with a clean tea towel. Allow to rise in the refrigerator overnight or for 40 minutes.

4. When you're ready to cook, put a few doughnuts in the Ninja Foodi air-fryer basket and fry them for 5–6 minutes, or until golden. As you cook the remaining doughnuts, remove from the basket and let cool on a wire rack. If you're concerned that the doughnuts will adhere to the basket and that indentations from the basket will develop on the doughnuts, you may insert a sheet of baking paper at the bottom of the basket.

5. The icing sugar should be sifted into a bowl and combined with the milk and vanilla essence while the last batch of cookies is baking. Put the glaze on the top of each doughnut when it has cooled. Allow the glaze to dry on the wire rack. Although it is best to consume it the same day, airtight containers may keep food fresh for up to 24 hours.

Per Serving :

Calories: 290 / fat: 7g / protein: 6g / carbs: 51g / Sodium:.37g

Air fryer baked potatoes

Prep:2 mins / Cook:50 mins / Serves 4

Ingredients

- 4 baking potatoes (about 250g each)
- ½ tbsp sunflower oil
- toppings of your choice, such as butter, cheese baked beans

Preparation Instructions

1. After washing the potatoes, pat them dry with paper towels. Transfer to a tray, sprinkle with oil, and then use your hands to thoroughly coat the potatoes in the oil. Add salt and pepper to taste; the salt will help the skins get crispy.
2. Put the potatoes in the ninja Foodi air fryer basket in a single layer. Potatoes should be cooked in the air fryer for 40 to 50 minutes, or until a sharp knife slides through them with ease, at 200°C. After 20 minutes, check the potatoes; if one side seems to be browning too quickly, flip them over with tongs. Then, after another 20 minutes, check the potatoes once more to make sure they are well cooked. When cooked, the interior should be fluffy and soft and the outside crisp. Split

Per Serving :

Calories: 206 / fat: 2g / protein: 5g / carbs: 40g / Sodium:0.01g

English breakfast

Prep:2 mins / Cook:50 mins / Serves 4

Ingredients

- Six mushrooms (15 minutes)
- Two sausages (12 minutes)
- Two tomatoes (11 minutes)
- Two rashers of bacon (10 minutes
- Half a can of baked beans (Six minutes)

- Two black puddings (Six minutes)
- Two eggs (Five minutes)

Preparation Instructions

1. Set your Ninja Foodi air fryer to 180 C for five minutes to pre-heat. Two eggs should be cracked and whisked into a ramekin. After adding, give the mushrooms and hash browns 15 minutes to cook. The sausages should be added with 12 minutes left. Add the tomatoes when there are 11 minutes left. Add the bacon with 10 minutes left on the clock. Add the black puddings and baked beans in a ramekin with six minutes left. Add the eggs with five minutes remaining.

2. To prevent an egg skin from forming, open the air fryer basket every two minutes and mix the eggs. Check your air fryer basket after the 15 minutes are up; certain items might need a little more time; leave those parts in and arrange the other dishes.

Per Serving :

Calories: 426 / fat: 32g / protein: 23g / carbs: 10g / Sodium:0.7g

Mini Blueberry Scones

Prep Time:15 mins / Cook Time: 15 mins / Total Time:30 mins / Servings: 8

Ingredients

- 250 ml all-purpose flour
- 1 ½ teaspoons baking powder
- ⅛ teaspoon salt
- 1 egg
- ½ teaspoon vanilla extract
- 2 teaspoons orange zest
- 4 tablespoons white sugar, divided
- ⅛ teaspoon baking soda
- 2 tablespoons butter
- 60 ml buttermilk
- 60 ml fresh blueberries

Preparation Instructions

1. The Ninja Foodi air fryer should be preheated to 360 degrees F. (180 degrees C).
2. In a larger bowl, combine the flour, 2 tablespoons sugar, baking powder, baking soda, and salt. Till the mixture resembles coarse crumbs, stir in the butter using two knives or a pastry blender.
3. In a small bowl, whisk the egg using a fork. Take 2 teaspoons of the egg and place it in a different small dish. The remaining egg is mixed with the buttermilk and vanilla extract using a fork. Add to flour mixture, stirring until slightly moistened. Add blueberries and gently mix.
4. Take the dough and place it on a lightly floured surface. Gently knead the dough for 8 to 10 strokes, or until it is no longer sticky. Form a 6-inch round out of the dough. Without separating, cut each piece into 8 wedges, dipping the knife in flour between each one.
5. In a separate dish, mix the remaining 2 tablespoons of sugar and orange zest. Sprinkle the sugar mixture on top of the dough and brush with the saved egg. Use a small, broad spatula

to carefully separate the dough wedges and set them in a single layer in the fryer basket, if required in batches. Cook scones for about 6 minutes, or until golden brown.

Per Serving :

Calories: 122 / fat: 4g / protein: 3g / carbs: 20g / Sodium:184mg

Air fryer sausages

Prep:2 mins / Cook:10 mins - 15 mins / Servings: 6

Ingredients
- 6 sausages of your choice

Preparation Instructions
1. Using a sharp knife, slice the sausages a few times all over. Put the sausages in the basket of your Ninja Foodi air fryer in a single layer.
2. The sausages should be cooked through after 10-15 minutes of cooking in the Ninja Foodi air fryer at 180°C and flipping every 5 minutes. Check if the meat has reached 75C in the centre if you have a meat thermometer. Serve with bread or as a side dish for breakfast.

Per Serving :

Calories: 120 / fat: 9g / protein: 6g / carbs: 4g / Sodium: 0.64g

Cornbread

Prep: 5 mins / Cook:15 mins / Servings: 6

Ingredients
- 1 Box Cornbread Mix
- 1 Large Egg
- 80 ml Semi Skimmed Milk

Preparation Instructions
1. Use a hand mixer to combine all the Ingredients in a bowl until the mixture forms a thick cornbread batter.
2. In a silicone round cake pan, pour the cornbread batter.
3. In the Ninja Foodi air fryer, place the cake pan, and air fry for 15 minutes at 180 °C/360 °F.
4. After letting it cool, take the cornbread out of the silicone and slice it before serving.

Per Serving :

Calories: 425 / fat: 13g / protein: 9g / carbs: 69g / Sodium: 761mg

Pigs in a Blanket

Prep: 5 mins / Cook:5 mins / Servings: 24

Ingredients

- 1 can 302.39 g) refrigerated crescent rolls
- 24 Lit'l Smokies fully cooked

Preparation Instructions

1. Your Ninja Foodi air fryer should be preheated to 325 degrees.
2. When the dough is unrolled, cut each triangle apart. Each triangle should be divided into three long pieces with one end the width of the smokies using a knife.
3. Place the smokies on the broad side, gently roll it up, and wrap each frank with a crescent-shaped seal.
4. Place the crescent-shaped smokies inside the basket of your air fryer after spraying the inside with cooking spray.
5. Cook the crescents for 5 minutes, or until golden brown.
6. If preferred, serve with ketchup and mustard for dipping.

Per Serving :

Calories: 60 / fat: 4g / protein: 1g / carbs: 4g / Sodium: 166mg

Air Fryer Cheese Swirls

Prep: 12 mins / Cook:12 mins / Servings: 6

Ingredients

- 2 Tbsp Mustard
- ½ Small Onion diced
- 150 g Grated Cheese
- Egg Wash
- Scone Dough
- 225 g Self Raising Flour
- 50 g Butter
- 120 ml Semi Skimmed Milk
- 28 g Grated Cheese
- 1 Tbsp Parsley
- Salt & Pepper

Preparation Instructions

1. Until the flour resembles breadcrumbs, work the fat into it. 28g of shredded cheese are added

along with your spices. then prepare a scone dough with just enough milk.

2. To a clean work surface and your rolling pin, add flour. Your dough should be rolled out into a large rectangle. Give the edges a mustard brush.
3. Then include grated cheese and onion chunks.
4. Roll it gradually starting at the top, adding egg wash along the way to help it stay together.
5. After rolling it completely, place it on a cutting board and cut it into medium-sized slices.
6. Sliced cheese whirls should be added to a layer of foil in the Ninja Foodi air fryer, which should then be air-fried for 6 minutes.

Per Serving :
Calories: 337 / fat: 33g / protein: 14g / carbs: 33g / Sodium: 639 mg

Fish Nuggets

Prep: 10 mins / Cook:8 mins / Servings: 2

Ingredients
- 2 Cod Fillets
- 2 Eggs beaten
- 480 ml Breadcrumbs
- 480 ml Plain Flour/All Purpose
- 2 Tbsp Lemon Juice
- 1 Tbsp Parsley
- 2 Tsp Dill Tops
- 2 Tsp Parsley
- 2 Tsp Basil
- Salt & Pepper
- Kitchen Gadgets
- Ninja Foodi Air Fryer
- Kitchen Towel

Preparation Instructions
1. Put the cod fillets on a kitchen towel and let the moisture absorb into the towels.
2. While you wait, build up your production line. In one dish, mix the beaten egg with the lemon juice, flour, and 1 tablespoon of parsley. In another bowl, combine the breadcrumbs with the remaining spice. Ensure that all of the bowls are thoroughly combined and arranged in the following order: flour, egg, breadcrumbs.
3. Cod fillets are set on a cutting board after being removed from the kitchen towel. Cut the meat into lengthwise and then widthwise slices after seasoning with salt and pepper.
4. Place the fish nuggets in the flour, then the egg, and then, using the other hand, into the breadcrumbs until thoroughly coated.
5. 8 minutes at 180 °C (360 °F) or until very crisp.

Chip Butty

Prep: 10 mins / Cook: 25 mins / Servings: 4

Ingredients

- 1 Tbsp Malt Vinegar
- Salt & Pepper
- Extra Virgin Olive Oil Spray
- 2 Tbsp Tomato Ketchup
- 8 Slices White Bread
- 6 Medium Potatoes
- ½ Tbsp Extra Virgin Olive Oil

Preparation Instructions

1. Put the peeled, sliced potatoes in a mixing bowl. Salt, pepper, vinegar, and extra virgin olive oil should all be added to the bowl with the potatoes after which they should be thoroughly mixed with your hands.
2. Cook the chips for 15 minutes at 160 c/320 f in the Ninja Foodi air fryer basket. When the chips are shaken, air fried them for 5 minutes at 180°C (360°F). Make sure they are fork tender by doing a fork test after that.
3. After that, pile your chips onto pieces of toast with butter.
4. Each scallop should be wrapped in bacon and anchored with a cocktail stick. Put them in the air fryer.
5. Over the chips, drizzle tomato ketchup. Afterward, cut it in half and serve.

Per Serving :

Calories: 635 / fat: 14g / protein: 19g / carbs: 107g / Sodium: 1227mg

Breakfast Frittata

Prep: 10 mins / Cook: 39 mins / Servings: 4

Ingredients

- 6 Reduced Fat Sausages sliced into quarters
- 1 Medium Zucchini/Courgette
- 2 Spring Onions sliced
- Salt & Pepper
- 240 ml Mascarpone
- 1 Large Sweet Potato
- 1 Tbsp Extra Virgin Olive Oil
- 1 Tsp Parsley
- 8 Large Eggs
- 200 g Grated Reduced Fat Cheddar

- Sliced Cherry Tomatoes optional   • Sprinkle Basil optional

Preparation Instructions

1. Sweet potatoes should be peeled and cut into pieces. Slice your zucchini into medium-sized pieces, then cut each piece into quarters. Combine the sweet potato and zucchini in a bowl with a tablespoon of extra virgin olive oil, parsley, salt, and pepper. Use your hands to stir.
2. Fill the Ninja Foodi air fryer basket with the zucchini and sweet potatoes, and air fry for 5 minutes at 180 °C (360 °F).
3. After shaking it, add the sausages, and air fry for an additional 12 minutes.
4. Fill the silicone plates with the filling Ingredients (zucchini, sweet potatoes, and some chopped spring onion).
5. With a fork, beat the eggs in a measuring cup before gradually adding the cream. Add parsley and salt and pepper to taste.
6. Spread the egg and cream mixture over the silicone after adding the shredded cheese. Sprinkle some basil on top and add some cherry tomato halves as garnish.
7. After placing the silicone in the Ninja Foodi air fryer, heat it for 17 minutes at 180°C (360°F) and then for 5 more at 170°C (340°F). The frittata is done if a cocktail stick inserted in the center of it comes out clean.
8. Remove the silicone from the frittata when it is cool enough to handle. then cut into quarters and store in the refrigerator so that you may have breakfast in a few days.

Per Serving :

Calories: 414 / fat: 30g / protein: 24g / carbs: 11g / Sodium: 902mg

Yorkshire Pudding Wrap

Prep: 2 mins / Cook: 4 mins / Servings: 2

Ingredients

- 400 g Leftover Roast Dinner
- 2 Giant Yorkshire Puddings frozen

Preparation Instructions

1. Use the Ninja Foodi air fryer to cook your frozen Yorkshire pudding for one minute at 180°C/360°F.
2. Use a rolling pin or your hand to flatten the Yorkshire pudding. Place a mixture of your leftovers in the Yorkshire pudding before putting it back in the air fryer.
3. Until piping hot, air fried for an additional 3 minutes at 180°C/360°F. To make your Yorkshire pudding into a wrap, fold it in half before consuming.

Per Serving :

Calories: 639 / fat: 21g / protein: 52.5g / carbs: 54g / Sodium: 112mg

Air Fryer Corned Beef Hash and Eggs

Prep: 5 mins / Cook: 13 mins / Servings: 2

Ingredients

- 300 g cooked potatoes cubed or refrigerated diced potatoes
- 120 g chopped onion
- 60 g cooked corned beef cubed
- Salt and pepper, to taste
- 1-2 Tablespoons bacon fat (or your preferred oil)
- 2 eggs

Preparation Instructions

1. Spray nonstick cooking oil on a cake pan that is just a little bit smaller than your Ninja Foodi air fryer basket. Aluminum foil may also be used to create a pan.
2. Fill the bottom with the remaining Ingredients and bacon grease. Season to taste. Stir to mix.
3. Cake pan should be placed in the Ninja Foodi air fryer basket and slid in. At 390 degrees, cook for 10 minutes.
4. Take the air fryer basket out and set it on a potholder. The corned beef hash mixture should have 2 wells.
5. Each one should contain an egg. To ensure that the egg is completely cooked, make sure it is at room temperature. Add salt and pepper to taste.
6. Set the ninja foodi air fryer to 370 degrees and add the basket. Depending on how well done you prefer your yolks, cook for 3–4 minutes. Continue cooking the egg, watching it every 30 seconds to ensure it doesn't overcook. The egg's top will start to become white, but the yolk will still be a little runny beneath.
7. Use a big spoon and a dish to scoop out one egg and the corned beef hash around it. Repeat for a second serving using the remaining egg and hash.

Per Serving :

Calories: 383kcal / Fat: 22g / Protein: 19g / Carbs: 27g / Sodium: 942mg

Air Fryer Shepherd's Pie

Prep: 15 mins / Cook: 45 mins / Servings: 6

Ingredients

- 2 tbsp butter
- 1/2 tsp salt
- 1 onion diced
- 220 g sliced mushrooms
- 1/2 tsp pepper
- 1 celery diced

- 1 carrot diced
- 2 cloves garlic minced
- 680 g ground beef
- 1 tbsp Worcestershire sauce
- 3 tbsp all-purpose flour
- 250 g shredded aged Cheddar cheese
- 2 tbsp finely chopped parsley
- 1 tbsp finely chopped fresh rosemary
- 2 tbsp tomato paste
- 350 ml sodium-reduced beef broth
- 1 tbsp Dijon mustard
- 1 kg frozen shredded hash browns
- 43 g grated parmesan cheese

Preparation Instructions

1. In the Ninja Foodi Air Fryer's inner pot, add butter. Select Saute and then set to High Temperature with the lid off. Add mushrooms along with 1/4 teaspoon each of salt and pepper. Cook the mushrooms for 3 to 5 minutes, or until they begin to brown.

2. Add the remaining salt and pepper, along with the onion, celery, carrot, rosemary, and garlic, and simmer for 2 to 3 minutes, or until softened. Ground beef is added and cooked for 3 to 5 minutes, or until it begins to brown. Cook for one minute after adding tomato paste.

3. Add the mustard, Worcestershire sauce, and broth and stir. Put a lid on the pot and tighten it to create a seal. set for 4 minutes on High Pressure.

5. Quick Release the pressure when the pressure cooking is finished. Release the pressure and take off the lid. Remove the cover and choose the Saute option with the High Temperature setting. Before adding it to the meat mixture, smoothly whisk the flour with 2 tablespoons of water. Cook for 2 to 3 minutes, or until thickened, after bringing to a boil.

6. Top with hash browns, Cheddar, and Parmesan cheese. The topping should be golden brown and bubbling after 25 to 35 minutes of roasting at 400°F using the Air Fryer Lid. Add a little parsley.

Per Serving :

Calories: 550 / Carbs: 35g / Protein: 34g / Fat: 30g / Sodium: 790mg

Beef Wellington

Prep: 40 mins / Cook: 40 mins / Servings: 2

Ingredients

- 2 tsp Dijon mustard
- 1 egg, lightly whisked
- Onion relish, to serve
- 1 sheet frozen puff pastry, just thawed
- Steamed broccolini, to serve
- 1 tbsp olive oil
- 2 x 3.5cm-thick (about 150g each) beef eye fillet steaks
- 200g button mushrooms, finely chopped
- 2 garlic cloves, crushed
- 2 French shallots, peeled, finely chopped
- 7 slices prosciutto

Preparation Instructions

1. In a big frying pan, heat the oil over high heat. Cook the steaks for 3–4 minutes on each

side, turning once, or until just lightly browned. Transfer to a platter and chill a little in the refrigerator.

2. heat to a medium level. Add shallot, garlic, and mushrooms to the pan. Cook for 15 minutes while stirring often, or until golden and liquid has evaporated. Place on a platter. Place in refrigerator for five minutes, or until just just cold.

3. On a piece of plastic wrap, arrange six slices of prosciutto, gently overlapping each other to form a rectangle. With a thin border, spread the mushie mixture over top. Place the steaks on top of the rectangle, lengthwise. Apply mustard on steaks. Overlap the steaks with the prosciutto. To fill up any gaps, place the remaining prosciutto slice lengthwise on top. Embrace ends. securely wrap with plastic wrap. Place in the refrigerator to cool for 20 minutes.

4. On a level surface, spread out the pastry. Unwrap the log, then place it on the crust. To enclose, fold pastry over and tuck ends under to seal. Place on a sheet of baking paper, seam-side down. After eggwashing the top, score the pastry diagonally with a knife.

5. Place in the basket of your Ninja Foodi air fryer. Cook until desired doneness is achieved, around 20 minutes at 180°C for medium rare. Serve with relish and broccolini.

Per Serving :
Calories: 4490 / Carbs: 56.9g / Protein: 56.8g / Fat: 70.2g / Sodium: 1.7g

Classic Briitsh Faggots

Prep: 20 mins / Cook: 60 mins / Servings: 4

Ingredients

- 1/2 teaspoon ground mace
- 2 tablespoons finely chopped fresh parsley
- 1 small red chili, seeded and finely chopped
- 4 110 grams pig's liver, coarsely chopped
- 4 110 grams bacon, coarsely chopped
- 1 medium onion, finely chopped
- Freshly ground pepper, to taste

- 1 teaspoon ground allspice
- 2 medium fresh sage leaves, finely chopped
- 4 110 grams pork shoulder, coarsely chopped
- 8 250 grams pork belly, coarsely chopped
- 4 110 grams breadcrumbs
- Salt, to taste
- 16 slices streaky bacon, or caul fat

Preparation Instructions

1. In a meat grinder, mince the pork shoulder, pig's liver, pork belly, and chopped bacon. As an alternative, finely chop the Ingredients in a food processor. Avoid overmixing.

2. Place the minced meat into a large bowl. Add the chile, onion, mace, allspice, parsley, sage, and breadcrumbs along with salt and pepper to taste. Completely combine.

3. Then, divide and shape the minced beef mixture into 8 balls of similar size using wet hands.

4. Two bacon pieces should be used to wrap each meatball tightly.

5. Place in your Ninja Foodi air fryer basket. 50 to 60 minutes at 160 F. Once done, take the food out of the oven and serve right away. Wrap the faggots if you are not yet ready to

consume them.

Per Serving :

Calories: 775 / Carbs: 27g / Protein: 57g / Fat: 47g / Sodium: 1.7g

Air Fryer Meatballs in Tomato Sauce

Prep: 5 mins / Cook: 8 mins / Servings: 4

Ingredients

- 1 tablespoon of Parsley, finely chopped
- 1 egg
- 60 g of Italian seasoned Breadcrumbs
- 450 g of Ground Beef
- 1 small Onion, finely chopped
- 2 fat cloves of Garlic, minced
- Salt and freshly cracked pepper, to taste
- 350 ml of Marinara Sauce (or any tomato based sauce of choice)

Preparation Instructions

1. Combine ground beef, finely minced onion, garlic, parsley, bread crumbs, an egg, and salt & pepper to taste in a big bowl. Be sure to thoroughly combine.
2. Form the mixture into 15 meatballs using a 2 inch ice cream scoop.
3. Place about 7 or 8 meatballs, one at a time, in the Ninja Foodi air fryer basket that has been lightly oiled. Give the meatballs a little oiling with a brush or spray. 8 minutes of air frying at 390 F.
4. The marinara sauce should be heated in a skillet while the meatballs are cooking. Throw the air-fried meatballs into the hot marinara sauce.
5. Serve hot with your preferred bread.

Per Serving :

Calories: 556 / Carbs: 21g / Protein: 47g / Fat: 11g / Sodium: 199mg

Steak & Ale Pie For Two In The Air fryer

Prep: 5 mins / Cook: 1 hr 35 mins / Servings: 2

Ingredients

- Shortcrust Pastry
- 500 g Beef Stewing Steak
- 1 Tbsp Plain Flour
- 2 OXO Cubes 1 beef and 1 vegetable

- 1 Can Ale
- 1 Large Onion peeled and diced
- 1 Tbsp Tomato Puree
- 1 Tbsp Olive Oil
- Salt & Pepper

Preparation Instructions

1. Put the onion, stewing beef, tomato puree, and olive oil in a big pan. Cook the meat until it is sealed on a medium heat.
2. Add the can of ale to a jug and fill it halfway with warm water. Add it to the pan along with the salt, pepper, and OXO cubes. The Ingredients are stirred before being heated all the way to a boil. Turn down the heat, then simmer for an hour.
3. Three tablespoons of warm water and one tablespoon of plain flour should be combined in a small bowl. You will have a thickening agent for your pie as a result. Slowly (a little at a time) pour it into the pan and thoroughly combine.
4. Remove the meat from the heat and set it aside.
5. Line your ramekins or tiny pot pie pans with the shortcrust pastry that you have rolled out. To prevent sticking, first lightly dust them with flour. Then add more pastry for the top before adding your pie filling. To give them a chance to breathe, stab them with a fork.
6. To get them to cook through in the centre, cook them in the Ninja Foodi Air Fryer for 10 minutes at 200°C and then for an additional 6 minutes at 170°C.

Per Serving :

Calories: 735kcal / Carbs: 8g / Protein: 44g / Fat: 57g / Sodium: 175mg

Chicken Spiedie

Prep: 8 mins / Cook: 30 mins / Servings: 4

Ingredients

- 1 Tbsp Olive Oil
- 1 Tbsp Basil
- Bread Rolls
- 1 Large Lemon
- Salt & Pepper

- 2 Tbsp Oregano
- Fresh Mint
- 2 Chicken Breasts
- 4 Garlic Cloves

Preparation Instructions

1. To begin, marinate your chicken. Chicken should be diced into large bits and placed in a mixing basin. Lemon juice should be squeezed into the dish. Add the garlic after peeling and slicing it thin. Olive oil and seasoning should be added. Use your hands to thoroughly combine until the chicken is well-coated. Place the chicken-filled skewers in the refrigerator for the night.

2. Make the bread next. Instead, shape our quick pull-apart bread into beautiful hotdog shapes. After making it, cook the four bread rolls in the Ninja Foodi Airfryer for 15 minutes at 185°C/365°F.
3. When they're finished, set them aside while you prepare the chicken. Additionally, cook the chicken at 185°C/365°F for 15 minutes.
4. Then put some homemade mayonnaise on top of the chicken before stuffing the bread rols, then serve.

Per Serving :

Calories: 172kcal / Carbs: 3g / Protein: 24g / Fat: 7g / Sodium: 132mg

Air fryer Chicken Parmesan

Prep: 2 mins / Cook: 12 mins / Servings: 15

Ingredients

- 2 Tbsp Coconut Butter
- 30 g Mozzarella Cheese
- 1 Tbsp Basil
- 100 g Spaghetti
- 2 Medium Chicken Breasts butterflied
- 1 Plain Flour

- 1 Tbsp Garlic Puree
- 50 g Parmesan Cheese
- 1 Tbsp Oregano
- 200 ml Homemade Tomato Sauce
- 3 Large Eggs
- Salt & Pepper

Preparation Instructions

1. Make your spaghetti first. Follow the directions on the packaging and boil it in a medium-sized pan. Drain the food once it has just finished cooking and brought to a boil. Put the coconut butter, salt, pepper, and garlic puree in the pan. Until the butter has melted and the garlic is combined, cook on medium heat. Mix the pasta with tongs in the coconut garlic butter. positioned aside.
2. Create your production line. In a bowl, whisk together three big eggs. Add your flour to a separate bowl and season with salt and pepper. Breadcrumbs are in a third bowl.
3. To prepare breadcrumbs, combine 1/3 of a loaf of bread with salt, pepper, oregano, and basil in a blender. Place it on a dish or bowl after it resembles breadcrumbs, then stir in the parmesan.
4. Chicken breasts should be rolled in flour, egg, and breadcrumbs in that order. Ensure that the chicken has a thick layer of breadcrumbs covering it.
5. Cook the chicken parmesan for 10 minutes at 180 °C (360 °F) in the air fryer. Add a layer of parmesan cheese after 10 minutes, then a layer of mozzarella cheese, and cook for an additional 2 minutes. Over the heated tomato sauce and noodles, serve the chicken parmesan.

Per Serving :

Calories: 505kcal / Carbs: 30.3g / Protein: 59g / Fat: 15.7g / Sodium: 262mg

Salisbury Steak Burgers

Prep: 2 mins / Cook: 12 mins / Servings: 2

Ingredients

- 3 Large Garlic Cloves
- 1 Tsp Worcester Sauce
- 500 g Minced Beef
- 2 Tsp Paprika
- Pinch Cayenne Pepper optional
- 1 Tsp Tomato Paste
- 2 Tsp Mustard Powder
- ½ Small Onion
- Salt & Pepper

Preparation Instructions

1. Slice the onion and garlic very thinly after peeling.
2. All of it should be placed in a mixing bowl.
Mix well, then shape into burger shapes.
3. Cook in your air fryer on the ninja foodi air fryer grill pan for 12 minutes at 160 c/320 f. Serve.

Per Serving :

Calories: 674kcal / Carbs: 7g / Protein: 44g / Fat: 51g / Sodium: 224mg

Boneless Pork Chops

Prep: 1 mins / Cook: 12 mins / Servings: 2

Ingredients

- 4 Boneless Pork Chops
- 2 Tsp Bouquet Garni
- 1 Tsp Pork Seasoning
- 12 Garlic Cloves
- 2 Tsp Oregano
- Salt & Pepper

Preparation Instructions

1. Use the bouquet garni, oregano, pork seasoning, salt, and pepper to season your pork chops.
2. Place the grill pan inside your air fryer, then place the pork chops on it.
3. Place peeled garlic cloves around the edge of the pork chops.
4. Serve the pork chops and garlic at 180°C/360°F for 12 minutes along with your preferred pork chop sides.

Per Serving :

Calories: 466kcal / Carbs: 11g / Protein: 60g / Fat: 19g / Sodium: 136mg

Roast Beef

Prep: 5 mins / Cook: 45 mins / Servings: 4

Ingredients
- 1 kg Beef Joint
- 1 Tbsp Extra Virgin Oliver Oil
- Salt & Pepper

Preparation Instructions
1. Remove the roast beef from its packaging, then massage it with extra virgin olive oil. Add salt and pepper to taste.
2. Place the roast beef, which has just been seasoned, on the rotisserie in the air fryer oven.
3. Make sure the meat is rotating before setting the timer for 45 minutes and the temperature to 190°C/380°F.
4. Double check to make sure it is cooked to medium-rare status after 45 minutes, and then slice.

Per Serving :

Calories: 666kcal / Protein: 43g / Fat: 54g / Cholesterol: 178mg / Sodium: 168mg

Pork Steak

Prep: 5 mins / Cook: 45 mins / Servings: 4

Ingredients
- 2 Pork Steaks
- Salt & Pepper

Preparation Instructions
1. Make sure your air fryer grill or air fryer basket is completely full before adding your air fryer pork steaks.
2. From within the Ninja foodi air fryer basket, season with salt and pepper.
3. After cooking for 8 minutes at 180°C/360°F, shut off the Ninja Foodi air fryer. Serve with your preferred side dishes for pork steak.

Per Serving :

Calories: 208kcal / Protein: 29g / Fat: 9g / Sodium: 64mg

Air Fryer Calamari Rings

Cook: 14 mins / Servings: 4

Ingredients

- 400 g Frozen Calamari Rings
- 2 Tsp Extra Virgin Olive Oil

Preparation Instructions

1. Calamari rings should be unwrapped before being placed in the air fryer basket.
2. 8 minutes of cooking at 180 °C/360 °F. Shake the inside of your air fryer basket, then cook for an additional 6 minutes at 200 C/400 F.
3. Serve with the seafood dipping sauce of your choice.

Per Serving :

Calories: 227kcal / Carbs: 28g / Protein: 4.6g / Fat: 11g

Fish Fingers In Air Fryer

Prep Time : 10 mins / Cook: 10 mins / Servings: 2

Ingredients

- 2 Tbsp Lemon Juice
- 2 Tsp Dill Tops
- 2 Eggs beaten
- 480 ml Plain Flour/All Purpose
- 2 Tsp Basil
- 1 Tbsp Parsley
- 2 Cod Fillets
- 480 ml Breadcrumbs
- 2 Tsp Parsley
- Salt & Pepper

Preparation Instructions

1. You should set the cod fillets on a dish towel so that the moisture may soak into the cloth.
2. Set up your production line while you wait. Combine the beaten egg, flour, lemon juice, and 1 tablespoon of parsley in a separate bowl. Combine the remaining spice with the breadcrumbs in a another dish. Make sure to fully combine all Ingredients and put them in this order: flour, egg, breadcrumbs.
3. Cod fillets are removed from the kitchen towel and put on a chopping board. After slicing lengthwise and generously season with salt and pepper, cut in half
4. Fish fingers should be well covered after being loaded into the flour, egg, and breadcrumbs with one hand.

5. Air fried for 10 minutes, or until nice and crispy, in your Ninja Foodi air fryer at 180°C/360°F.

Per Serving :

Calories: 1733kcal / Carbs: 182g / Protein: 196g / Fat: 18g / Sodium: 2179mg

AIR FRYER WHITE FISH

Prep time: 5 MINS Cook: 10 mins / Servings: 2

Ingredients

- 340 g tilapia filets , or other white fish (2 filets each)
- kosher salt or sea salt , to taste
- fresh cracked black pepper , to taste
- fresh chopped parsley
- 2.5 g garlic powder
- 2.5 g lemon pepper seasoning
- 2.5 g onion powder , optional
- lemon wedges

Preparation Instructions

1. For five minutes, preheat the Ninja Foodi Air Fryer to 360°F. The fish filets should be rinsed and dried with paper towels. Add salt, pepper, garlic powder, lemon pepper, and/or onion powder after spraying or coating with olive oil. Repeat on the other side.
2. Lay perforated baking paper inside the air fryer's base to prevent sticking. Spray the paper very lightly.
3. Over the paper, place the fish. Next to the fish, place a couple lemon slices.
4. Fish may be split with a fork after 6 to 12 minutes of air-frying at 360°F. The thickness, coldness, and personal liking of the filets will determine the timing.
5. Serve the heated dish with the toasted lemon wedges and a sprinkle of minced parsley, if desired.

Per Serving :

Calories: 169kcal / carbs: 1g / protein: 34g / fat: 3g /sodium: 89mg

Frozen Shrimp Fajitas

Prep time: 3 MINS Cook: 8 mins / Servings: 1

Ingredients
- 1 White Onion
- 2 Tbsp Fajitas Seasoning

- 250 g Frozen Shrimp peeled and cooked
- 300 g Mixed Peppers
- Salt & Pepper

Preparation Instructions

1. Slice your peppers and white onion after peeling and dicing them.
2. Combine the peppers, onion, fajita spice, and frozen shrimp in a mixing dish.
3. With your hands, mix everything in the bowl until it is evenly distributed.
4. Fill the Ninja Foodi air fryer with your shrimp fajitas, and cook for 8 minutes at 180 °C/360 °F. Serve.

Per Serving :

Calories: 354kcal / Carbs: 24g / Protein: 55g / Fat: 4g / Sodium: 1956mg

Air Fryer Fishcakes

Prep time: 10 MINS Cook: 35 mins / Servings: 4

Ingredients

- Cook The Fish
- 300 g Baby Potatoes
- Salt & Pepper
- 1 Pink Salmon Fillet
- 1 Pollock Fillet
- Salt & Pepper
- 2 Tbsp Lemon Juice
- 2 Eggs beaten
- 480 ml Plain Flour/All Purpose
- 2 Tsp Parsley
- Salt & Pepper
- 1 Red Onion peeled and diced
- 2 Tsp Parsley
- 1 Tbsp Fresh Parsley shredded
- 1 Tbsp Butter
- Cook The Potatoes
- 2 Tsp Extra Virgin Olive Oil
- 2 Tsp Butter
- 1 Cod Fillet
- 2 Tsp Dill
- Make The Production Line
- 1 Tbsp Parsley
- 480 ml Breadcrumbs
- 2 Tsp Dill Tops
- 2 Tsp Basil
- Make The Fishcakes
- 2 Tsp Coriander
- 2 Tsp Thyme
- Salt & Pepper

Preparation Instructions

1. The mixed fish fillets should be placed in a bowl and allowed to sit for an hour to drain any excess liquid. If they are frozen, you may thaw them in the bowl first.
2. After that, take out the fish and set it on a cutting board without the extra water. Add dill, pepper, and salt to taste.
3. Place the fish in the air fryer and cook for 8 minutes at 180°C/360°F. After that, place the fish in a bowl and flake it with a fork.

4. Add baby potatoes, extra virgin olive oil, salt, and pepper to another bowl. Use your hands to combine for an even coat. 17 minutes at 180 c/360 f in the air fryer, then mash with a little butter. Cooked potatoes with the mash.

5. Mash the potatoes thoroughly with a fork or a masher, and then, if you think it needs it, add some butter. Then, after it is safe to touch, form fish patties.

6. Set up your production line though while you're waiting for them to cool. The beaten egg, lemon juice, flour, and 1 tablespoon of parsley are combined in one bowl; the breadcrumbs and other spices are combined in another. Ascertain that the flour, egg, and breadcrumbs bowls are in that order and that they are all thoroughly combined.

7. Once your patties are ready, load them into the flour, egg, and breadcrumbs, giving each a thorough coating. Fill the Ninja Foodi air frying basket with the ingredients, then air fry for 10 minutes at 180°C/360°F, or until everything is cooked through and has the consistency of crispy breadcrumbs.

Per Serving :

Calories: 874kcal / Carbs: 107g / Protein: 69g / Fat: 17g / Sodium: 1032mg

Air Fryer Tempura Shrimp

Cook: 8 mins / Servings: 2

Ingredients

- Olive Oil Spray
- 12 Frozen Tempura Shrimp

Preparation Instructions

1. Frozen tempura shrimp should be placed in the Ninja Foodi air fryer basket.
2. Spray extra virgin olive oil on the dish for additional crispness.
3. For eight minutes at 180°C/360°F, air fry tempura.
4. Your perfectly crispy tempura shrimp are now prepared for serve.

Per Serving :

Calories: 352kcal / Carbs: 27.3g / Protein: 6.5g / Fat: 23.8g

Air Fryer Scallops

Prep Time : 5 mins / Cook: 12 mins / Servings: 2

Ingredients

- 500 g Frozen Raw Scallops
- 2 Lemons

- 6 Garlic Cloves
- 1 tbsp Fresh Parsley
- Salt & Pepper

Preparation Instructions

1. Place the frozen scallops in the air fryer basket after removing them from the package and draining any extra liquid. Add salt and pepper to taste. Fill the air fryer with chopped parsley, peeled garlic cloves, and lemon wedges.
2. Turn you Ninja Foodi Air fryer At 180°C/360°F, air fried for 12 minutes.
3. Then, make sure a scallop is firm and has begun to turn light brown.
4. Then put the scallops on a dish, sprinkle the lemon juice over them, and serve.

Per Serving :

Calories: 218kcal / Carbs: 21g / Protein: 32g / Fat: 2g / Sodium: 985mg

Air Fryer Tuna Steak

Prep Time : 5 mins / Cook: 7 mins / Servings: 2

Ingredients

- 125 g Cherry Tomatoes
- 2 Tsp Basil
- 1 Tsp Thyme
- 1 Tsp Oregano
- 2 Tuna Steaks
- 1 Tbsp Extra Virgin Olive Oil
- Salt & Pepper

Preparation Instructions

1. Slice the cherry tomatoes in half, add extra virgin olive oil, salt, pepper, and basil, and toss to combine.
2. Add tuna steaks to the Ninja Foodi air fryer basket after seasoning with salt, pepper, oregano, and thyme. Fill up the spaces with cherry tomatoes.
3. After 7 minutes of cooking at 190 c/380 f. Check to see if the tuna steak is done. Cook for a further two minutes at the same temperature if necessary. In such case, if your tuna steaks are quite thick, repeat this procedure.
4. Then, for a quick, light meal, serve the tuna steaks beside the cherry tomatoes.

Per Serving :

Calories: 322kcal / Carbs: 3g / Protein: 40g / Fat: 15g / Sodium: 74mg

Air Fryer Cod Loin Fillets

Prep Time : 5 mins / Cook: 10 mins / Servings: 2

Ingredients
- 2 Cod Loin Fillets
- 150 g Cherry Tomatoes halved
- 1 Tsp Oregano
- 1 Tsp Thyme
- 2 Tsp Basil
- 1 Tsp Parsley
- Salt & Pepper

Preparation Instructions
1. Your cod fillets should be placed on a kitchen towel so that the moisture may absorb into the towels.
2. After removing the kitchen towel, set the cod fillets on a cutting board. Everything save the basil should be well-seasoned. then fill the air fryer basket.
3. Fill in the spaces with cherry tomatoes and season with basil.
4. Cod fillets are air-fried for 10 minutes at 180°C/360°F.
5. When the air fryer beeps serve your cod and tomatoes.

Per Serving :
Calories: 755kcal / Carbs: 4g / Protein: 161g / Fat: 6g / Sodium: 495mg

Vol Au Vent Cases

Prep Time : 10 mins / Cook: 10 mins / Servings: 2

Ingredients
- 1 kg Frozen Puff Pastry
- 1 Large Egg beaten
- 200 g Frozen Large Prawns
- 3 Tbsp Cocktail Sauce
- 2 Tsp Chives
- Salt & Pepper

Preparation Instructions
1. Make sure your puff pastry is at room temperature and completely defrosted. Flour your rolling pin and puff pastry with flour.
2. Your pastry should be rolled out before being cut into 18 circles with a medium cookie cutter.

3. Set aside 9, then use a tiny cookie cutter to cut the remaining 9 again, removing the middles as you go. Now you have nine medium pastry circles and nine little circles that resemble miniature doughnuts.
4. Place the circles over the first nine, then egg wash them. The circles will then adhere to them with the aid of the egg wash.
5. Place over a sheet of foil in Ninja foodi the air fryer after a second egg wash.
6. In the Ninja Foodi air fryer, for eight minutes at 180°C/360°F, then let cool while you make the filling. The fillings should then be added to the vol au vents if you're making them ahead of time before placing them on the buffet or in the refrigerator.

Per Serving :
Calories: 644kcal / Carbs: 51g / Protein: 13g / Fat: 43g / Sodium: 355mg

Air Fryer Shrimp Tacos

Prep Time : 10 mins / Cook: 8 mins / Servings: 4

Ingredients
- 250 g Frozen Shrimp peeled and precooked
- 3 Tbsp Sour Cream
- 1 Lime juice only
- Salt & Pepper
- 2 Large Avocados
- 1 Spring Onion
- 1 Tsp Cumin
- 1 Tbsp Paprika
- 1 Lime into wedges
- 1 Tbsp Salsa
- 1 Small Red Onion
- ¼ Medium Red Cabbage
- Taco Sauce Seasonings
- 2 Tbsp Mexican
- ½ Tsp Cayenne Pepper
- 1 Garlic Clove

Preparation Instructions
1. Garlic and red onion should be peeled and diced. Red cabbage should be washed and shredded. Your spring onion should be cleaned and cut. Slice and peel the avocados.
2. Put the frozen shrimp and lime wedges in the Ninja Foodi air fryer basket, and cook for 7 minutes at 180°C/360°F.
3. Garlic, half fo red onion, and half an ofavocado should all be added to a blender. One lime's juice, sour cream, a fourth of the cabbage that has been chopped up, 90% of the Ingredients listed above (save some for the shrimp), salt, and pepper. Pulse until the mixture becomes a creamy avocado sauce.
4. Remove the shrimp from the air fryer when it beeps, place them in a bowl, add the salsa and additional ingredients, and combine with a fork.
5. Spread taco sauce over your tacos, add shrimp, add more sauce, and then cover with your leftovers to make yummy toppings and then serve.
6. 8 minutes at 180°C/360°F in the Ninja Foodi air fryer, followed by cooling while you prepare

the filling. Then, if you're creating the vol au vents ahead of time, add your fillings before setting them on the buffet or in the refrigerator.

Per Serving :

Calories: 302kcal / Carbs: 21g / Protein: 17g / Fat: 19g / Sodium: 578mg

Cajun Shrimp

Prep Time : 2 mins / Cook: 6 mins / Servings: 2

Ingredients

- 30 Frozen Shrimp
- ½ Tsp Extra Virgin Olive Oil
- 1 Tbsp Cajun Seasoning
- 1 Tsp Garlic Puree
- Salt & Pepper
- 1 Lemon juice only
- 1 Tsp Cajun Seasoning optional

Preparation Instructions

1. Frozen shrimp should be counted out and taken out of the freezer bag. Add your cajun spice, extra virgin olive oil, salt, pepper, and garlic to a mixing bowl.
2. Place in the Ninja Foodi air fryer basket after tossing. 180°C/360°F for 6 minutes of cooking.
3. Add more cajun seasoning and lemon juice once the food has finished cooking.

Per Serving :

Calories: 125kcal / Carbs: 7g / Protein: 19g / Fat: 3g / Sodium: 703mg

Air Fryer Lamb Steaks

Prep Time : 5 mins / Cook: 10 mins / Servings: 4

Ingredients

- 4 Lamb Steaks
- 2 Tsp Honey
- 1 Tsp Frozen Chopped Garlic
- Salt & Pepper
- Fresh Mint

- 2 Tsp Lemon Juice
- 1 Tsp Thyme
- 2 Tsp Extra Virgin Olive Oil

Preparation Instructions

1. On a cutting board, arrange your lamb steaks and season with salt, pepper, and dried thyme.
2. Two teaspoons of fresh mint should be finely chopped and added to a bowl with everything else except the lamb. Mix well and then spoon over your lamb steaks. Allow the steaks to marinade in the refrigerator for one hour.
3. Add more fresh mint to the Ninja Foodie air fryer basket before adding the steaks.
4. At 180°C/360°F, air fry for 10 minutes.

Per Serving :

Calories: 315kcal / Carbs: 3g / Protein: 42g / Fat: 14g / Sodium: 100mg

Fillet Steak

Prep Time : 2 mins / Cook: 8 mins / Servings: 2

Ingredients

- 12 oz Fillet Steak
- Pinch Garlic Powder
- Salt & Pepper

Preparation Instructions

1. Add salt, pepper, and garlic spice to your steaks, if desired.
2. Your fillet steaks should be placed in the Ninja Foodi air fryer basket.
3. Air fried for 4 minutes at 180°C/360°F, flip, season the other side once more, and air fry for 4 more minutes at the same temperature.
4. Serve with potato wedges.

Per Serving :

Calories: 354kcal / Protein: 34g / Fat: 24g / Sodium: 88mg

Air Fryer Whole Chicken

Prep Time : 2 mins / Cook: 1 hr 5 mins / Servings: 4

Ingredients

- 1.5 kg Frozen Medium Whole Chicken
- Extra Virgin Olive Oil Spray
- Salt & Pepper

Preparation Instructions

1. Place the breast side up in the air fryer basket with your frozen entire chicken. To almost defrost, air fry for 20 minutes at 80 c/160 f.
2. Spray all exposed skin with extra virgin olive oil, then add salt and pepper to taste. At 180 c/360 f, air fried for a further 25 minutes. Use a fork to flip the chicken over.
3. Spray one more, then season with salt and pepper.
4. Once fully done, continue to air fry for another 20 minutes at 180°C/360°F.

Per Serving :

Calories: 387kcal / Protein: 33g / Fat: 27g / Sodium: 126mg

T Bone Steak

Prep Time : 2 mins / Cook: 18 mins / Servings: 2

Ingredients

- 820 g Thick T Bone Steak
- 2 Tsp Sweet Paprika
- 2 Tsp Parsley
- Salt & Pepper

Preparation Instructions

1. Your t-bone steak should be placed on a clean cutting board and let to settle to room temperature.
2. Salt, pepper, and half of the parsley and sweet paprika should be used to season the T-bone steak.
3. T-bone steak should be loaded into the Ninja Foodi air fryer and cooked for 9 minutes at 180°C/360°F.
4. T-bone should be turned over, seasoned once more, and air-fried for another 9 minutes at the

same temperature. When you cut it open, it will be either rare or medium-rare.

Per Serving :

Calories: 916kcal / Carbs: 1g / Protein: 85g / Fat: 61g / Sodium: 223mg

Turkey Thighs

Prep Time : 10 mins / Cook: 1 hr 2 mins / Servings: 4

Ingredients

- 1.1 kg Large Turkey Thigh
- 1 Gravy Boat Turkey Gravy
- 1 Tbsp Rosemary
- 100 g Frozen Brussel Sprouts
- 150 g Frozen Parsnips
- 4 Air Fryer Stuffing Balls
- 1 Tbsp Extra Virgin Olive Oil
- 1 Tbsp Chicken Seasoning
- 150 g Frozen Roast Potatoes
- Salt & Pepper

Preparation Instructions

1. Put a turkey thigh in the Ninja Foodi air fryer basket and add extra virgin olive oil to smooth it out. Afterward, season the food generously with salt, pepper, and rosemary. 30 minutes of cooking at 180 °C/360 °F.
2. After 30 minutes, fill up the spaces with frozen parsnips, roast potatoes, and sprouts and continue cooking for a further 20 minutes at the same temperature.
3. Take out the vegetables, put them in a serving dish, then flip the turkey thigh when the air fryer sounds. Fill up the spaces with stuffing balls and turkey gravy, and cook for an additional 12 minutes at the same temperature.
4. Optional. Reheat the sides for 4 minutes at 160°C/320°F while the turkey is resting and being cut into slices. Enjoy after serving.

Per Serving :

Calories: 537kcal / Carbs: 17g / Protein: 54g / Fat: 27g / Sodium: 1221mg

Air Fryer Brisket

Prep Time : 5 mins / Cook: 45 mins / Servings: 4

Ingredients

- 1.2 kg Beef Brisket
- 2 Tsp Rosemary
- 1 Tbsp Extra Virgin Olive Oil
- Salt & Pepper
- 2 Tsp Parsley
- 2 Tsp Thyme
- 2 Tsp Basil

Preparation Instructions

1. The simplest way to season your beef brisket and collect any particles of spice that have come off is to place it in a tray.
2. Smoother after adding extra virgin olive oil, and smoother after adding spices. As the beef cooks, the dry spices will adhere to the oil and remain on the meat.
3. Roll the meat in the tray to collect any stray spice that may fall off.
4. After placing the Ingredients in the Ninja Foodi air fryer basket, cook for 30 minutes at 180 c/360 f.
5. Cook for a final 15 minutes at the same temperature after flipping. Now, it will be a medium.

Per Serving :

Calories: 497kcal / Carbs: 1g / Protein: 62g / Fat: 26g / Sodium: 237mg

Prime Rib

Prep Time : 5 mins / Cook: 1 hr / Servings: 4

Ingredients

- 2 kg Prime Rib
- 1 Tbsp Extra Virgin Olive Oil
- 1 Tsp Garlic Powder
- Salt & Pepper

Preparation Instructions

1. Cut the prime rib to match your air fryer's dimensions and place it on a spotless cutting board. If it has a bone in, take it out and save the bone for beef stock, gravy, soup, stew, etc.
2. Smoother after adding extra virgin olive oil, and smoother after adding spices. As the beef cooks, the dry spices will stick to the oil and remain on the meat.
3. Overnight, wrap in foil and marinate in the refrigerator.
4. Remove the foil the following day and place it in the Ninja Foodi air fryer basket. Push down with your fingertips to prevent the top of the rib roast from burning if it's touching the top too much. Cook for 30 minutes without preheating the air fryer at 180°C/360°F.
5. Cook for 20 minutes at the same temperature after turning. This time, it will be a medium rare. If you want your meat medium rare, remove it now.
6. The rib roast should be turned again over and cooked for an additional 10 minutes at the same temperature for medium to well done.
7. After that, move it to a cutting board to rest before cutting and serving. Be aware that your cutting board will be covered with fluids, so have some kitchen towels on hand.

Per Serving :

Calories: 1016kcal / Carbs: 1g / Protein: 45g / Fat: 91g / Sodium: 149mg

Air Fryer Pork Roast

Prep Time : 10 mins / Cook: 1 hr 20 mins / Servings: 4

Ingredients

- 1.2 kg Pork Shoulder
- 1 kg Air Fryer Sweet Potato Cubes
- 1 Tbsp Olive Oil
- 1 Tbsp Parsley
- 1 tsp Garlic Powder
- Salt & Pepper

Preparation Instructions

1. Use square slits of a similar size to score the pork roast. Apply extra virgin olive oil as a mist. Add salt, pepper, and any additional Ingredients to the pork before cooking.
2. Make sure the rod has passed through both ends of the pork shoulder before inserting it. Each side's clamps should be secured.
3. Make sure it is secure before placing it in the Ninja Foodi air fryer oven. Time and temperature should be set at 1 hour and 180 C/360 F, accordingly. Remove from the air fryer and rest when it beeps.
4. Remove the clamps and rod when it has rested for about 5 minutes, then let it sit without cutting for another 5 minutes.

Per Serving :

Calories: 520kcal / Carbs: 51g / Protein: 40g / Fat: 17g / Sodium: 278mg

Lamb Kofta Kebabs

Prep Time : 5 mins / Cook: 16 mins / Servings: 4

Ingredients

- 500 g Ground Minced Lamb
- 1 Tsp Mixed Herbs
- 1 Tsp Coriander
- 1 Tsp Chilli Flakes
- Salt & Pepper
- 1 Tsp Cumin
- ½ Tsp Tandoori Seasoning
- 1 Tsp Mixed Spice
- 1 Tsp Turmeric

Preparation Instructions

1. Put the kofta Ingredients in a bowl and thoroughly combine with your hands.
2. Make kebabs in the form of thick sausages.
3. Place immediately into the Ninja Foodi air fryer basket or onto kebab skewers. ensuring

that they have space to cook without sticking and are not touching one another. 8 minutes of cooking at 180 °C/360 °F.

4. Before serving, turn the food over and cook for a further 8 minutes at the same temperature.
5. Serve hot with flatbreads and your favorite dipping sauce.

Per Serving :

Calories: 362kcal / Carbs: 1g / Protein: 21g / Fat: 30g / Sodium: 83mg

Air Fryer Rump Steak

Prep Time : 2 mins / Cook: 15 mins / Servings: 1

Ingredients

- 1 Rump Steak
- 1 Tsp Garlic Powder
- Salt & Pepper

Preparation Instructions

1. Put the rump steak in the basket of your Ninja Foodi air fryer. Add salt, pepper, and garlic powder for seasoning. 7 minutes of air frying at 140 C/280 F.
2. Turn your rump steak over and season it one more when it beeps. Cook at the same temperature for a further 8 minutes. Serve.

Per Serving :

Calories: 480kcal / Carbs: 2g / Protein: 46g / Fat: 32g / Sodium: 119mg

Duck Breast

Prep Time : 5 mins / Cook: 20 mins / Servings: 2

Ingredients

- 250 g Air Fryer Duck Fat Potatoes
- 1 Tsp Parsley

- 2 Duck Breasts
- Salt & Pepper

Air Fryer Duck Marinade:

- 1 Tbsp Extra Virgin Olive Oil
- 1 Tsp Dried Garlic
- ½ Tsp Balsamic Vinegar

- ½ Tsp French Mustard
- 2 Tsp Honey

Preparation Instructions

1. Cook your duck fat potatoes until they are halfway done.
2. Duck breasts should be scored and seasoned with parsley, salt, and pepper. After combining

the ingredients, brush the marinade mixture on the duck breasts.

3. Your duck breasts are covered with potatoes that have been fried in duck fat. Cook for 20 minutes at 180 C/360 F. Slice, then present.

Per Serving :

Calories: 693kcal / Carbs: 45g / Protein: 49g / Fat: 35g / Sodium: 757mg

Air Fryer Pot Roast

Prep Time : 5 mins / Cook: 1 hr / Servings: 4

Ingredients

- 1.2 Kg top round roast/topside
- 5 Medium Potatoes
- 4 Tbsp Maple Syrup
- 1 Tbsp Extra Virgin Olive Oil
- 1 Tbsp Soy Sauce
- 4 Tbsp Worcester Sauce
- 4 Large Carrots
- Salt & Pepper

Preparation Instructions

1. Give your beef roast a light score. Add half of the Worcester sauce and the soy sauce to the meat. Make sure the spice goes into the scored areas before adding salt and pepper. Prepare the food in the Ninja Foodi air fryer basket for 15 minutes at 180 °C (360 °F).
2. Peel and cube your carrots and roast potatoes as they are cooking. Add the loaded Ingredients to a bowl along with the remaining Worcester sauce, maple syrup, olive oil, more salt, and pepper.
3. Add the potatoes and carrots to the spaces when the air fryer beeps.
4. Cook at 160c/320f for a further 45 minutes. Slice after 5 minutes of resting before serving.

Per Serving :

Calories: 546kcal / Carbs: 23g / Protein: 68g / Fat: 19g / Sodium: 630mg

Acorn Squash

Prep Time : 5 mins / Cook: 15 mins / Servings: 2

Ingredients

- 2 Acorn Squash
- Savoury Acorn Squash
- 1 Tsp Oregano
- Sweet Acorn Squash
- 2 Tsp Cinnamon
- 1 Tbsp Honey
- 1 Tsp Basil
- Extra Virgin Olive Oil Spray
- 1 Tsp Nutmeg
- Salt & Pepper

Preparation Instructions

1. Slice your acorn squash lengthwise after trimming the end. Take the seeds out.
2. Spray extra virgin olive oil on the flesh.
3. Then add salt, pepper, basil, and oregano for the savory seasoning. Then, at 180°C/360°F, air fry for 15 minutes.
4. Sweet acorn squash should be air-fried for 10 minutes at 180°C/360°F with nutmeg and half the cinnamon.
5. After the ten minutes, add honey and the remaining cinnamon to the center of the acorn. A last 5 minutes of air frying are done at the same temperature.
6. Next, whether it's anything sweet or savory, test it with a fork before serving.

Per Serving :

Calories: 217kcal / Carbs: 56g / Protein: 4g / Fat: 1g / Sodium: 14mg

Air fryer Asparagus

Cook: 11 mins / Servings: 2

Ingredients

- 250 g Asparagus
- Salt & Pepper
- Extra Virgin Olive Oil Spray
- 8 g Butter
- 30 g Grated Cheese

Preparation Instructions

1. Cut the asparagus's bottoms, then season with salt and pepper.

2. Make sure they fit in the air fryer basket before adding, and then drizzle with extra virgin olive oil. 8 minutes of air frying at 180°C/360°F.
3. In the Ninja Foodi air fryer basket, remove the asparagus and cover with a layer of foil. Reintroduce the asparagus and season with shredded cheese and tiny pieces of butter.
4. Before serving, continue to air fry for a further 3 minutes at 200c/400f.

Per Serving :

Calories: 118kcal / Carbs: 5g / Protein: 9g / Fat: 8g / Sodium: 260mg

Air Fryer Halloumi Salad

Prep Time : 5 mins / Cook: 6 mins / Servings: 2

Ingredients

- 225 g Halloumi
- ½ Medium Red Onion
- 2 Tsp Oregano
- Halved Cherry Tomatoes
- 4 Tsp Extra Virgin Olive Oil for drizzling
- 150 g Mixed Olives
- 200 g Rocket Leaves
- Sliced Cumber
- Extra Virgin Olive Oil Spray

Preparation Instructions

1. Slice your halloumi into cubes and season with oregano.
2. Halloumi should be placed in the Ninja Foodi air fryer. 6 minutes of air frying at 180°C/360°F.
3. Make your salad while the air fryer is doing its thing. Clean rocket leaves are the base, followed by sliced cucumber along the sides, halved cherry tomatoes, olives, and finally some chopped red onion in the center.
4. When the air fryer beeps add a drizzle of extra virgin olive oil and add the air fryer halloumi chunks. Serve whilst the halloumi is still warm.

Per Serving :

Calories: 575kcal / Carbs: 11g / Protein: 29g / Fat: 48g / Sodium: 2549mg

Air Fryer Zoodles

Prep Time : 5 mins / Cook: 13 mins / Servings: 2

Ingredients

- 4 Medium Zucchini
- 2 Tsp Extra Virgin Olive Oil
- 1 Tbsp Basil
- Extra Virgin Olive Oil Spray
- 1 Tsp Garlic Puree
- 1 Tbsp Oregano
- Salt & Pepper

Preparation Instructions

1. To make zucchini noodles, use a spiralizer or julienne peeler.
2. Place the zucchini in a bowl and top with the extra virgin olive oil and spices.
3. Turn your Ninja Foodi air fryer, for 8 minutes of air frying at 180°C/360°F.
4. Spray extra virgin olive oil on the air fryer zoodles, shake, and cook for an additional 5 minutes at 200°C (400°F).

Per Serving :

Calories: 113kcal / Carbs: 15g / Protein: 5g / Fat: 5g / Sodium: 33mg

Teriyaki Vegetables

Prep Time : 5 mins / Cook: 19 mins / Servings: 2

Ingredients

- 1 Small Broccoli
- 1 Mixed Pepper
- 1 Tbsp Extra Virgin Olive Oil
- Salt & Pepper
- 4 Mushrooms
- 1 Medium Zucchini/Courgette
- 2 Tsp Chinese Five Spice
- 3 Tbsp Healthy Teriyaki Sauce

Preparation Instructions

1. Your vegetables should be cut up and diced before being added to a mixing bowl. Add salt, pepper, and Chinese five spice. oil of extra virgin olives in a bowl. Add to the ninja foodi air fryer basket after thoroughly mixing.
2. 14 minutes of air frying at 180°C/360°F.
3. With your hands, remove the vegetables from the bowl and add them back in. Next, add the teriyaki sauce, mix well, and then transfer to a sheet of foil. Rearrange in the air fryer and cook for an additional 5 minutes at 180 C/360 F.

Per Serving :

Calories: 240kcal / Carbs: 34g / Protein: 14g / Fat: 9g / Sodium: 1148mg

Air Fryer Lentil Burgers

Prep Time : 5 mins / Cook: 17 mins / Servings: 8

Ingredients

Instant Pot Green Lentils
- 1 Tsp Basil
- 1 Tsp Thyme
- 1 Tsp Harissa
- 1 Tsp Oregano
- 1 Tsp Paprika
- 1 Large Sweet Potato

- 6 Medium Carrots
- 50 g Gluten Free Oat Flour
- Salt & Pepper
- 1 Small Red Onion
- 1 Tsp Garlic Puree

Preparation Instructions

1. Your sweet potato and carrots should be peeled, diced, and pressure cooked for 5 minutes to make sure they are tender and simple to mash. Add the green lentils, the sweet potatoes, the carrots, and all the spices to the inner pot of the instant pot. Add the red onion, which has been peeled and finely diced.
2. When you get a texture like standard beef burger patties, mash everything together with your hands. Roll in oats after forming into patties for hamburgers. Four lentil burgers should be placed on foil in the Ninja foodi air fryer.
3. Cook for a further 12 minutes at 200°C/400°F after turning the food over.

Per Serving :

Calories: 77kcal / Carbs: 16g / Protein: 2g / Fat: 1g / Sodium: 58mg

Harvest Casserole

Prep Time : 5 mins / Cook: 20 mins / Servings: 2

Ingredients

- 100 g Fresh Sprouts
- 2 Green Apples
- 3 Slices Thick Bacon chopped into bits
- ½ Medium White Onion
- 2 Tbsp Thyme
- 2 Red Apples
- 4 Sausages
- 1 Medium Sweet Potato
- 1 Tbsp Extra Virgin Olive Oil
- Salt & Pepper

Preparation Instructions

1. Apples should be peeled and cut into cubes. Your sweet potato should be peeled and cut into cubes, as well as your onion. Your sprouts should be cleaned and quartered.
2. Add thyme, extra virgin olive oil, salt, and pepper to a bowl. Use your hands to combine the spice and oil until you have a decent coating.
3. Place the food inside the Ninja foodi air fryer and cook for 8 minutes at 180 °C (360 °F).
4. Slice your sausages into medium-sized pieces and chop your bacon into bacon bits while the air fryer is working its magic. Shake the basket and place the sausage and bacon on top when the air fryer sounds. Cook at the same temperature for ten minutes.
5. Shake the air fryer and combine the fruit and vegetables with the sausage and bacon. Before serving, cook for an additional 2 minutes at 200 c/400 f.
6. Alternately, increase the cook time by 7 minutes rather of 2, and spritz with extra virgin olive oil for crispier results.

Per Serving :

Calories: 1123kcal / Carbs: 81g / Protein: 37g / Fat: 74g / Sodium: 1509mg

Air Fryer Baked Potato

Prep Time : 5 mins / Cook: 38 mins / Servings: 2

Ingredients

- 6 Medium White Potatoes
- 1 Tbsp Extra Virgin Olive Oil
- 3 Cans Tinned Tuna
- 3 Tbsp Mayonnaise
- 2 Tbsp Butter
- Salt & Pepper
- 100 g Frozen Corn
- 50 g Grated Cheese

Preparation Instructions

1. Prepare the baked potatoes. With a fork, prick the potatoes on the top, bottom, and sides. Add salt and pepper and rub with extra virgin olive oil. Place Ingredients in the Ninaj Foodi air fryer basket.
2. At 200°C (400°F), baked potatoes are air-fried for 20 minutes. After rotating, the other side should continue to cook for an additional 15 minutes.
3. Put the baked potato toppings in order. Mayonnaise, drained canned tuna, and softened frozen corn should all be combined in a dish.
4. Combine baked potatoes. Open the cooked potatoes, fill with butter, tuna, and sweet corn, then sprinkle cheese on top. Reload and let the cheese melt in the air fryer basket. This may be accomplished with a fast 3-minute cook time at the same temperature.

Per Serving :

Calories: 358kcal / Carbs: 34g / Protein: 24g / Fat: 15g / Sodium: 426mg

Frozen Broccoli And Cauliflower

Prep Time : 5 mins / Cook: 8 mins / Servings: 2

Ingredients

- 300 g Frozen Cauliflower
- 300 g Frozen Broccoli Florets
- 1 Tbsp Extra Virgin Olive Oil
- Salt & Pepper
- Parmesan optional

Preparation Instructions

1. In your instant pot inner pot, add a cup of water.
2. Frozen broccoli and cauliflower should be added to your steamer basket.

3. Add salt and pepper to your liking.

A cover ought to be on the instant pot. Cook for 0 minutes after sealing the valve.

4. Immediately after it beeps, remove the pressure and put your frozen, drained broccoli and cauliflower in the Ninja foodi air fryer basket.

5. Increase the amount of salt and pepper in the dish. Spray the veggies with extra virgin olive oil to make them crispier.

6. 8 minutes of cooking at 180°C/360°F. Serve.

Per Serving :

Calories: 150kcal / Carbs: 17g / Protein: 7g / Fat: 8g / Sodium: 95mg

Zucchini Vegetarian Meatballs

Prep Time : 5 mins / Cook: 10 mins / Servings: 4

Ingredients

- 2 Cups Gluten Free Oats
- 40 g Feta Cheese crumbled
- 1 Tsp Lemon Rind
- 1 Tsp Dill
- Salt & Pepper

- 150 g Zucchini
- 1 Large Eggs beaten
- 6 Basil Leaves thinly sliced
- 1 Tsp Oregano

Preparation Instructions

1. Your Ninja Foodi air fryer should be set to 400°F/200°C.

Grate the zucchini first, then press the grated zucchini between your hands into a bowl to remove any remaining water.

2. In a mixing dish, combine the squeezed-out zucchini with the beaten egg. The remaining ingredients—all save the oats—should be added.

3. Combine the squeezed-out zucchini and the beaten egg in a mixing bowl. All of the other Ingredients should be added, excluding the oats.

4. Oats should resemble fine breadcrumbs after being blended on the highest speed in a blender. Because they will quickly thicken, oats should be put to the bowl a bit at a time.

6. Make bite-sized meatballs out of the mixture.

7. Place in the air fryer and cook for 10 minutes at 200 °C (400 °F). Serve.

Per Serving :

Calories: 203kcal / Carbs: 29g / Protein: 9g / Fat: 6g / Sodium: 133mg

Air Fryer Zucchini Fritters

Prep Time : 5 mins / Cook: 6 mins / Servings: 4

Ingredients

- 100 g Plain Flour
- 1 Medium Egg beaten
- 5 Tbsp Milk
- 150 g Grated Courgette
- 75 g Spring Onion thinly sliced
- 25 g Cheddar Cheese grated
- 1 Tbsp Mixed Herbs
- Salt & Pepper

Preparation Instructions

1. Set the Ninja foodi air fryer to 180°C/360°F to preheat. Grate the zucchini making sure to remove any excess moisture.
2. In a bowl with the plain flour, add the spices. Before adding the milk and egg to the flour, mix the two Ingredients together to create a smooth, creamy batter. Toss in the cheese. Include the zucchini and spring onions. Mix thoroughly.
3. If the batter isn't very thick, add additional flour and cheese until it is a batter that is roughly the thickness of a pancake.
4. After forming them into miniature hamburgers, place them in the Ninja Foodi Air Fryer. Cook for 6 minutes, or until well cooked, at 180°C/360°F.
5. Serve them with plenty of mayonnaise on the side.

Per Serving :

Calories: 164kcal / Carbs: 23g / Protein: 7g / Fat: 5g / Sodium: 69mg

Vegan Veggie Balls

Prep Time : 5 mins / Cook: 12 mins / Servings: 4

Ingredients

- 200 g Cauliflower
- 70 g Carrot
- 2 Tsp Garlic Puree
- 1 Tsp Paprika
- 2 Tsp Oregano
- 1 Cup Gluten Free Oats

- 100 g Sweet Potato
- 90 g Parsnips
- 1 Tsp Chives
- 1 Tsp Mixed Spice
- ½ Cup Desiccated Coconut
- Salt & Pepper

Preparation Instructions

1. Any surplus water from your cooked vegetables should be squeezed onto a fresh tea towel.
2. They are combined with the spices in a bowl. Combining well, then forming into medium-sized balls For two hours, place them in the refrigerator so they may begin to firm up.
3. In a blender, combine your coconut and gluten-free oats until the mixture resembles coarse

flour. Put some in a bowl.

4. You should place the vegetable balls in the grill pan of the Ninja Foodi air fryer after dipping them in the mixture.

5. 10 minutes of 200 °C/400 °F cooking. The dish should be turned over and cooked for a further 2 minutes at the same temperature on the other side. Serve.

Per Serving :

Calories: 213kcal / Carbs: 31g / Protein: 6g / Fat: 9g / Sodium: 49mg

Meatless Veggie Bites

Prep Time : 5 mins / Cook: 20 mins / Servings: 16 bites

Ingredients

- 1 Large Broccoli
- 6 Large Carrots
- ½ Cauliflower made into cauliflower rice
- 1 Small Courgette
- 1 Can Coconut Milk
- 1 cm Cube Ginger peeled and grated
- 1 Tbsp Olive Oil
- 1 Tbsp Coriander
- 1 Tsp Cumin

- 1 Large Cauliflower
- Handful Garden Peas
- 1 Large Onion peeled and diced
- 2 Leeks cleaned and thinly sliced
- 50 g Plain Flour
- 1 Tbsp Garlic Puree
- 1 Tbsp Thai Green Curry Paste
- 1 Tbsp Mixed Spice
- Salt & Pepper

Preparation Instructions

1. Cook the onion in a pan with the garlic, ginger, and olive oil until the onion is well-colored.

2. Cook the onion in a pan with the garlic, ginger, and olive oil until the onion is well-colored.

3. Cook your veggies (apart from the courgette and leek) for 20 minutes or until they are almost done while you steam your onion.

4. In the skillet, add the courgette, leek, and curry paste. Cook for an additional 5 minutes at medium heat.

5. Add the cauliflower rice after thoroughly combining the remaining spice and coconut milk. Stir one more, then boil for 10 minutes.

6. Add the cooked veggies after it has simmered for 10 minutes and the sauce has reduced by half. You now have a nice basis for your veggie snacks after thoroughly combining.

7. Place in the refrigerator for one hour to chill.

8. Make into bite-sized pieces and fry in the air fryer after an hour. Cook at 180°C for 10 minutes, then serve with a dip to chill things up.

Per Serving :

Calories: 117kcal / Carbs: 12g / Protein: 2g / Fat: 7g / Sodium: 39mg

Stuffed Mushrooms

Prep Time : 5 mins / Cook: 8 mins / Servings: 16 bites

Ingredients

- 16 oz Mini/Baby Portobello Mushrooms
- 1 lb Mild Ground Pork Sausage Cooked and Drained
- 8 oz Package of Cream Cheese Softened
- 2 Tbsp Fresh Chopped Parsley
- 1 Garlic Clove Crushed
- 1/4 Cup Grated Parmesan Cheese

Preparation Instructions

1. Take off the stems and clean the mushrooms. In a food processor, add the stems.
2. The food processor should be filled with the cooked sausage, cream cheese, parsley, garlic clove, and cheese. Blend until the Ingredients are well chopped.
3. Apply olive oil cooking spray on the foil or air fryer basket.
4. Place each mushroom on the foil or basket after stuffing it. Apply a second application of cooking spray evenly.
5. 8 minutes of cooking at 390 degrees in the air fryer. Remove and serve with care.

Per Serving :

Calories: 105kcal / Carbs: 2g / Protein: 5g / Fat: 9g / Sodium: 205mg

French Toast Sticks

Prep Time : 5 mins / Cook:8 mins / Servings: 4

Ingredients

- 5 Slices Bread
- 180 ml Semi Skimmed Milk
- 1 Tsp Cinnamon
- Extra Virgin Olive Oil Spray
- 2 Large Eggs
- 1 Tsp Vanilla Essence
- Pinch of Nutmeg
- Icing Sugar optional

Preparation Instructions

1. Crack the eggs into a bowl, then whisk in the milk and seasonings.
2. Cut the bread into sticks.
3. Or, if you prefer bite-sized French toast, cut each stick into two or three pieces, depending on

the length.

4. One at a time, place toast sticks in the bowl, covering both sides.
5. To prepare your Ninja Foodi air fryer, spray extra virgin olive oil inside of it and then use a pastry brush to paint the interior.
6. The air fryer basket should be filled with French toast sticks, which should be fried for 4 minutes at 180°C/360°F.
7. After turning, continue to cook the other side for a further 4 minutes at the same temperature. Sprinkle with confectioners' sugar just before serving.

Per Serving :

Calories: 142kcal / Carbs: 18g / Protein: 7g / Fat: 4g / Sodium: 202mg

CHICKEN WINGS

Prep Time : 5 mins / Cook: 25 mins / Servings: 4

Ingredients

- 450 g chicken drumettes and flats
- salt and pepper to taste
- One homemade recipe of buffalo sauce (optional)

Preparation Instructions

1. Ninja Foodi air fryer should be preheated to 380 degrees.
2. Cut or separate the flat and drumette of each chicken wing at the joint, if required. Get rid of the tips.
3. With a towel, dry the chicken wings; you want them to be as dry as possible so they will crisp up.
4. On the chicken wings, liberally sprinkle salt and pepper.
Shake the basket or rotate the wings halfway through cooking to guarantee equal cooking. Cook wings at 380 degrees for 20 to 22 minutes.
5. The chicken wings should be cooked for 4-5 minutes, or until the outsides are attractively crispy, at 400 degrees after turning up the air fryer's temperature.
6. Apply buffalo sauce or the sauce of your choice.

Air fryer crab cakes

Prep Time : 5 mins / Cook: 10 mins / Servings: 4

Ingredients

- 220 g lump crab meat
- 3 green onions, chopped
- 1 red bell pepper, de-seeded and chopped
- 3 tablespoons mayonnaise

- 3 tablespoons breadcrumbs
- 1 teaspoon lemon juice
- 2 teaspoons Old Bay Seasoning

Preparation Instructions

1. Set the temperature of your Ninja foodi air fryer to 370 degrees.
2. Just before serving, combine the lump crab meat, pepper, green onions, mayonnaise, breadcrumbs, Old Bay Seasoning, and lemon juice on a large dish.
3. Gently form four equal-sized crab patties. The liquids included in lump crab meat should be kept as much as possible.
4. Each crab cake needs to be carefully put into the hot air fryer after being covered with a paper ring.
5. Cook the fresh crab cakes in the air fryer for 8 to 10 minutes, or until the crust is golden.
6. Remove the air fryer's crab cakes and serve them with your preferred sauce and more lemon, if you want.

AIR FRYER FROZEN MOZZARELLA STICKS

Prep Time : 6 mins / Cook: 6 mins / Servings: 4

Ingredients

- 10 frozen mozzarella sticks
- marinara sauce for dipping

Preparation Instructions

1. Set the air fryer to 360 degrees of heating.
2. In the Ninja foodi air fryer, cook the frozen mozzarella sticks for 6 to 8 minutes.
3. Pinch softly (and with caution, since they are hot). When the mozzarella stick gives and the cheese inside is soft, they are finished.
4. Take them out of the air fryer and serve them with marinara sauce on the side2. Frozen mozzarella sticks should be cooked for 6 to 8 minutes in the Ninja foodi air fryer.
3. Slightly pinch (and with caution, since they are hot). They are done when the mozzarella stick yields and the inside cheese is soft.
4. When you are ready to serve them, remove them from the air fryer and add some marinara sauce to the side.

Loader tater tots

Prep Time : 8 mins / Cook: 8 mins / Servings: 3

Ingredients

- 450 g tater tots
- 1 to 1/2 teaspoons bacon bits
- 64 g shredded cheddar cheese
- 2 green onions, chopped

- sour cream drizzled on top (optional)

Preparation Instructions

1. You should warm your air fryer at 400 degrees.
2. Cooking tater tots for 7-9 minutes while shaking the pan halfway through is recommended.
3. Put fried tater tots. in an air fryer pan.
4. Add shredded cheddar cheese, chopped bacon, and green onions.
5. Melt the cheese for 1-2 minutes after the Ninja foodi air fryer reaches 350 degrees.
6. Pour some sour cream over top, if preferred.

Air Fryer Garlic Mushrooms

Prep Time : 5 mins / Cook: 9 mins / Servings: 3

Ingredients

- 250 g Button Mushrooms
- Fresh Rosemary
- ½ Tsp Garlic Powder
- 1 Tbsp Butter optional
- 1 Garlic Bulb
- Extra Virgin Olive Oil Spray
- Salt & Pepper

Preparation Instructions

1. Place the mushrooms on a clean cutting board, then cut each into thirds along their length. Sprinkle your mushrooms with salt, pepper, and garlic powder. Peel the garlic bulb to get numerous garlic cloves after that.
2. Put fresh rosemary, garlic, and mushrooms in the Ninja foodi air fryer basket. Spray with extra virgin olive oil and air fry for 6 minutes at 180°C/360°F.
3. Spray extra virgin olive oil on once again and cook for an additional 3 minutes at 200 °C (4 °F).
4. Use the microwave to reheat some butter, or wait until the air fryer has finished cooking before using it. Then, just before serving, stir the mushrooms in the butter.

Per Serving :

Calories: 82kcal / Carbs: 5g / Protein: 4g / Fat: 6g / Sodium: 57mg

Sausage Rolls

Prep Time : 15 mins / Cook: 10 mins / Servings: 4

Ingredients

- 150 g Air Fryer Pie Crust
- 2 Tsp Oregano
- Egg Wash optional
- 450 g Sausage Meat
- Salt & Pepper

Preparation Instructions

1. Make your pie crust first. Add mixed herbs to the crust to enhance the flavor. Roll out onto a clean work surface or chopping board.
2. Next, cover the dough with a thick coating of sausage meat. Egg wash the sides before folding it up and slathering it with egg wash. Remove any excess ends.
3. You should put your sausage roll in the ninja foodi air fryer.
4. Air fry for 10 minutes at 200°C/400°F before serving.

Per Serving :

Calories: 518kcal / Carbs: 19g / Protein: 20g / Fat: 40g / Sodium: 869mg

Air Fryer Zucchini Fries

Prep Time : 5 mins / Cook: 10 mins / Servings: 4

Ingredients

- 2 medium zucchini
- 100 g almond flour or panko/Italian breadcrumbs
- 1 teaspoon Italian seasoning or seasoning of choice
- Pinch of salt and pepper

- 1 large egg beaten
- 100 g parmesan cheese grated
- ½ teaspoon garlic powder optional
- Oil for spraying olive or oil of choice

Preparation Instructions

1. Slice the zucchini into three- to four-inch long, half-inch thick sticks.
2. In a small bowl, add almond flour (or bread crumbs), grated parmesan, herbs, and a dash of salt and pepper. blend Combining.
3. After dipping the zucchini in the egg and almond flour mixture, place it on a dish or baking sheet. Spray the zucchini with cooking spray liberally.
4. Working in batches, place the zucchini fries in the Ninja Foodi air fryer in a single layer. then fry for 10 minutes at 400F until crispy.

Per Serving :

Calories: 147kcal / Carbs: 6g / Protein: 9g / Fat: 10g / Sodium: 224mg

Jalapeno Poppers

Prep Time : 10 mins / Cook: 5 mins / Servings: 5

Ingredients

- 10 fresh jalapenos
- 32 g shredded cheddar cheese
- cooking oil spray

- 170 g cream cheese I used reduced-fat
- 2 slices bacon cooked and crumbled

Preparation Instructions

1. To generate two halves per jalapeño, cut each one in half vertically.
2. In a bowl, place the cream cheese. Everything will soften in the microwave for 15 seconds.
3. Remove the seeds from the jalapeño and inside. If you want your poppers to be hot, save some of the seeds.
4. In a bowl, mix the cream cheese, bacon bits, and shredded cheese. Mix thoroughly.
5. Add some of the seeds mentioned above to the cream cheese mixture and thoroughly combine for poppers that are really fiery.

Place a piece of the cream cheese mixture into each jalapeño.

6. Place the poppers inside the Air Fryer from Ninja Foodi. Spray some frying oil on the poppers.
7. Close the Air Fryer. Cook the poppers on 370 degrees for 5 minutes to 8 minutes.
8. Remove from the Air Fryer and cool before serving.

Per Serving :

Calories: 62kcal / Carbs: 3g / Protein: 3g / Fat: 4g

Air Fryer Crispy Shrimp

Prep Time : 10 mins / Cook: 20 mins / Servings: 4

Ingredients

- 32 g flour
- ½ teaspoon garlic powder
- 43 gcup seasoned bread crumbs
- 2 large eggs beaten
- 340 g large shrimp with tails peeled and deveined

- 1 ½ teaspoons lemon pepper seasoning
- ½ teaspoon salt or to taste
- 43 g cup Panko bread crumbs

- cooking spray

Preparation Instructions

1. Combine half of the spices with the flour. Combine the remaining spices with the bread crumbs in a separate bowl.
2. For five minutes, heat the air fryer to 400°F. Add shrimp to the flour mixture and toss. A shrimp should be taken out of the flour mixture and dipped in the egg, followed by the breadcrumb mixture. Repeat with the rest of the shrimp.
3. Apply cooking spray sparingly to the shrimp. Shrimp should be added to the air fryer basket in a single layer. 4 minutes to cook.
4. Cook for a further 4 minutes, or just until cooked through and crispy, then turn the shrimp over. Cooking spray should be used.
5. Repeat with the rest of the shrimp. Serve with cocktail sauce.

Per Serving :

Calories: 210 / Carbs: 17g / Protein: 24g / Fat: 4g / Sodium: 1158mg

Air Fryer Crispy Tofu

Prep Time : 5 mins / Cook: 10 mins / Servings: 2

Ingredients

- 250 g Natural Tofu
- 1 Tbsp Garlic Puree
- 1 Tbsp Basil
- Salt & Pepper
- 60 ml Lemon Juice
- 1 Tbsp Parsley
- 1 Tbsp Harissa

Preparation Instructions

1. Slice the tofu into long pieces after removing it from the container. The tofu should be covered with a thick tea towel before being set onto a large casserole dish. Set the tofu aside for two hours while it is being pressed to remove its moisture.
2. Combine the lemon juice and garlic purée in a bowl.
3. Add the remaining Ingredients to another bowl and combine thoroughly.
4. Place the tofu on a cutting board and discard the tea towels and casserole dish when the two hours are over. Put the lemon and garlic in after cutting into cubes.
5. Then, after thoroughly coating every piece of tofu, add the dry rub. Put the food in the Ninja Foodi air fryer basket and cook it there for 6 minutes at 180 °C (360 °F).
6. Shake the air fryer and cook for a further 4 minutes at 200c/400f and then serve.

Per Serving :

Calories: 132kcal / Carbs: 9g / Protein: 12g / Fat: 6g / Sodium: 108mg

Sweet Potato Wedges

Prep Time : 5 mins / Cook: 20 mins / Servings: 4

Ingredients

- 3 Large Sweet Potatoes
- 2 Tsp Paprika
- 1 Tsp Parsley
- 2 Tsp Extra Virgin Olive Oil
- 2 Tsp Cajun
- Salt & Pepper

Preparation Instructions

1. You should clean the skins of your sweet potatoes. You should peel and chop your sweet potatoes into wedges.
2. In a bowl, thoroughly blend the extra virgin olive oil, spices, and sweet potatoes using your hands.

3. The basket of your Ninja foodi air fryer should be filled with sweet potato wedges, which should then be fried for 15 minutes at 160 °C (320 °F).
4. Heat for an extra five minutes at 200 C/400 F after checking the wedges with a fork and shaking the air fryer basket to ensure they are done.

Per Serving :

Calories: 172kcal / Carbs: 35g / Protein: 3g / Fat: 3g / Sodium: 95mg

Air Fryer Crumpets

Cook: 3 mins / Servings: 2

Ingredients

- 4 Crumpets
- 2 Tsp Strawberry Jam optional
- 2 Tsp Chicken Liver Pate optional
- 2 Tsp Butter
- 2 Tsp Soft Cheese optional
- Salt & Pepper

Preparation Instructions

1. The Ninja foodi air fryer basket can hold up to four crumpets at once, but make sure they are not piled on top of one another. 180°C/360°F for 2 minutes should be the air fryer's temperature and cooking time settings, accordingly.
2. When the air fryer beeps, add butter to the top and cook for an additional minute at 200°C/400°F.
3. As the butter seeps into the crumpets' cracks, serve.

Per Serving :

Calories: 346kcal / Carbs: 58g / Protein: 10g / Fat: 8g / Sodium: 586mg

Carrot Chips

Prep Time : 5 mins / Cook: 15 mins / Servings: 2

Ingredients

- 6 Medium Carrots
- 2 Tsp Oregano
- Salt & Pepper
- 28 g Parmesan Cheese optional
- 1.5 Tsp Extra Virgin Olive Oil
- 2 Tsp Thyme
- 1 Tbsp Maple Syrup optional

Preparation Instructions

1. You should rapidly wash your carrots after cutting them into chips.
2. In a bowl, mix the carrots, extra virgin olive oil, and spices.

3. Using the Ninja Foodi air fryer basket, cook for 15 minutes at 180 c/360 f.

4. Add maple syrup and parmesan cheese before serving.

Per Serving :

Calories: 190kcal / Carbs: 26g / Protein: 7g / Fat: 7g / Sodium: 352mg

Garlic Bread

Prep Time : 5 mins / Cook: 15 mins / Servings: 4

Ingredients

- 500 g Bread Maker Pizza Dough
- 1 Tsp Parsley
- Salt & Pepper
- 2 Tbsp Extra Virgin Olive Oil
- 2 Tsp Garlic Puree

Preparation Instructions

1. Start by loading your bread maker with a batch of pizza dough. You may also use leftover bread.
2. Mix the toppings after adding them to a ramekin.
3. L lay out the dough into two pizza pans when your bread machine beeps.
4. Spread out the pizza dough with a fork before adding the ramekin's contents to it and spreading it out evenly. Use the Ninja Foodi air fryer and cook the meal for 10 minutes at 160°C (320°F).

Per Serving :

Calories: 384kcal / Carbs: 60g / Protein: 7g / Fat: 11g / Sodium: 588mg

Cheese Quiche

Prep Time : 15 mins / Cook: 18 mins / Servings: 4

Ingredients

- 300 g Air Fryer Pie Crust
- 4 Cherry Tomatoes
- 3 Large Eggs
- 2 Tsp Mixed Herbs
- 300 g Grated Cheddar Cheese
- 75 ml Whole Milk
- 1 Tbsp Oregano
- Salt & Pepper

Preparation Instructions

1. Make your pie crust first. Add mixed herbs to the crust to enhance the flavor. Roll out into ramekins or other like containers.
2. Salt and pepper are added while you combine the milk and eggs in a mixing dish.

3. When the ramekins are little more than 3/4 full, pour the milk and egg mixture over the cheese that has been shredded. The mixture should be topped with cherry tomatoes that have been sliced in half. Oregano and more cheese should be included as well.

4. The suggested air-frying duration is 8 minutes at 180°C/360°F, followed by another 10 minutes at 160°C/320°F.

Per Serving :

Calories: 715kcal / Carbs: 40g / Protein: 29g / Fat: 49g / Sodium: 830mg

Cheese & Ham Stromboli

Prep Time : 25 mins / Cook: 12 mins / Servings: 4

Ingredients
- Bread Maker Pizza Dough
- 400 g Grated Cheese
- 300 g Leftover Ham
- 2 Tbsp Pizza Sauce
- 1 small Egg beaten

Preparation Instructions
1. Load up your bread maker pizza dough Ingredients and get it started.
2. Get your cheese grated.Prep your pizza sauce and shred your ham.   Make a rectangle out of your rolled-out pizza dough. Pizza sauce, shredded cheese, and ham are all added to the pizza dough.
3. Make a stromboli out of your pizza.
4. To help the stromboli breathe, make a few tiny cuts all over. Apply egg wash to the top and sides.
5. Cook for 12 minutes at 160 c/320 f after loading the Nija foodi air fryer basket.

Per Serving :

Calories: 560kcal / Carbs: 5g / Protein: 54g / Fat: 35g / Sodium: 2450mg

Calzone

Prep Time : 5 mins / Cook: 10 mins / Servings: 4

Ingredients
- 500 g Pie Crust
- Egg Wash optional
- 300 g Turkey Pot Pie Leftovers

Preparation Instructions

1. To cut out calzone shapes, roll out your pie crust and use the back of it. Each pie dough I roll out generally yields four.
2. A pie maker should be topped with one of the pie crust circles. Pie filling should be placed to one of the edges, pressed down, and checked to make sure there isn't too much.
3. The pies will be removed from the pie maker after the other side has been pressed down and placed down. Repeat this process for each pie you are baking.
4. Cover your pie crust with egg wash. Place your calzone into the Ninja foodi air fryer basket and cook for 10 minutes at 180c/360f.
5. Cook for 12 minutes at 160 c/320 f after loading the Nija foodi air fryer basket.

Per Serving :

Calories: 670kcal / Carbs: 61g / Protein: 18g / Fat: 39g / Sodium: 539mg

Sweet & Sour Chicken Balls

Cook: 12 mins / Servings: 2

Ingredients

- Frozen Chicken Balls
- 1 Tsp Extra Virgin Olive Oil
- Frozen Sweet & Sour Sauce

Preparation Instructions

1. The air fryer basket should be filled with frozen sweet and sour chicken balls.
2. 180°C/360°F for 8 minutes of cooking. Shake the chicken balls in the air fryer and add the sweet and sour sachet as well.
3. Your chicken balls should be lightly coated with olive oil. To help your chicken balls get crispier, cook for an additional 4 minutes at 200c/400f.
4. Serve with the sauce of your choice.

Per Serving :

Calories: 303kcal / Carbs: 26.6g / Protein: 24g / Fat: 10.3g

Quesadilla

Prep Time : 4 mins / Cook: 6 mins / Servings: 2

Ingredients

- 8 Tortilla Wraps
- Egg Wash
- 100 g Grated Mexican Cheese
- 3 Tbsp Salsa

Cheese Quesadilla Filling:

- 2 Tbsp Sour Cream
- 1 Tbsp Mexican Seasoning
- 1 Cup Frozen Sweetcorn
- 2 Tsp Garlic Powder
- 1 Can Black Beans
- 250 g Grated Frozen Cheddar Cheese

Preparation Instructions

1. Put the Ingredients for the filling in a bowl and stir them with a fork until well combined.
2. You should stuff one of your tortilla wraps full of the filling.
Add some cheese shreds on top.
3. Spread salsa with a knife over another wrap, then add shredded cheese to create a sandwich.
4. Fill the top with sticks and egg wash it to keep the sticks from moving.
5. After filling the Ninja Foodi air fryer, cook for 4 minutes at 180 °C/360 °F.
6. After the beep, take out the cocktail sticks, rotate, and apply more egg wash. Cook for a further 2 minutes at 200c/400f.
7. Slice and serve with extra salsa. Rinse and repeat until you have used all your tortilla wraps and are out of filling.

Per Serving :

Calories: 590kcal / Carbs: 45g / Protein: 28g / Fat: 34g / Sodium: 1077mg

Air fryer Hot Cross Buns

Prep Time : 10 mins / Cook: 16 mins / Servings: 9

Ingredients

Buns:
- 1/2 cup raisins or dried cranberries
- 1 cup hot water
- 3/4 tablespoons dry instant yeast about 1 packet
- 3/4 cup warm milk divided
- 1/2 cup granulated sugar and 1/2 teaspoon
- 4 tablespoon butter unsalted & room temperature
- 3 large eggs room temperature, and divided
- 1/2 teaspoon kosher salt
- 3 1/2 cup all-purpose flour
- 1/4 teaspoon ground cinnamon
- 1/4 teaspoon ground clove
- 1/4 teaspoon ground nutmeg

For the Glaze:
- 1/2 cup powdered sugar
- 1 1/2 teaspoon milk
- 1 teaspoon orange or lemon juice

Preparation Instructions

1. A small baking pan that will fit within the air fryer basket should be greased and placed aside.
2. Orange juice, milk, and powdered sugar should be combined until a thick frosting forms. Pour for later use into a zip-top bag.
3. Rinse the raisins after soaking them in the hot water for 10 to 15 minutes.
4. Mix the instant yeast, sugar, and 1/4 cup of the heated milk in a separate small bowl or glass measuring cup. After 10 minutes of resting, the mixture should be foamy and the yeast should have doubled in size.
5. Add the remaining milk, sugar, butter, and salt to a large bowl or stand mixer. Mix until the mixture is smooth, either by hand or with an electric mixer.
6. Add two of the eggs, which have been beaten, to the butter mixture. Pour the cinnamon, clove, and nutmeg first, then the yeast mixture.
7. Use your mixer's dough hook now, and add the flour one cup at a time to the egg mixture. Knead the dough on a low pace until all the flour is integrated and it turns smooth and somewhat sticky.
8. The plump raisins or cranberries should be dried using a paper towel before being added into the dough. Put the dough in a bowl that has been greased, and then cover it with a towel. Give the dough time to rise for 45 to 60 minutes, or until it has doubled in size.
9. Cut the dough in half and place it on a lightly dusted board. Divide the halves, and then use the dough to shape 12 uniform balls. The 12 dough balls should be placed on a cutting board or pan and covered with the moist towel to rise once more for 30 to 40 minutes.
10. Place six rolls into the baking pan that has been buttered. Cook the rolls in your air fryer for 5 minutes at 315F. Beat the remaining egg with a teaspoon of water in the meanwhile. Remove the basket from the fryer when the five minutes are up and give the bun tops a wash. Depending on your air fryer and pan size, go back and cook for an additional three to five minutes. Return the buns to the fryer for an additional 2-4 minutes, or until cooked through, if the middle is still doughy.
11. Take out of the fryer and let cool. After they have cooled, use an icing bag with a little tip cut off and pipe crosses onto the tops of each bun. Plate, serve, and enjoy!

Per Serving :

Calories: 234kcal / Carbs: 47g / Protein: 6g / Fat: 2g / Sodium: 130mg

Pizza Rolls

Prep Time : 5 mins / Cook: 10 mins / Servings: 4

Ingredients

- 500 gPizza Dough
- 4 Tbsp Pizza Sauce
- 150 g Hard Cheese

- 50 g Grated Gouda
- 8 Tsp Soft Cheese
- 2 Tsp Oregano
- 1 Tsp Basil
- Egg Wash optional

Preparation Instructions

1. Roll out your pizza dough and using a pizza cutter, cut it into 8 equal pizza slices.
2. Layer it with pizza sauce, a teaspoon of soft cheese and stick your hard cheese to it. Add some grated cheese too.
3. Roll it from the biggest to the smallest part until you have 8 croissant shaped pizza rolls. Cover the tops with egg wash.
4. Place the pizza rolls into a baking tray and add the baking tray to the middle shelf of your air fryer oven. Cook at 180c/360f for 10 minutes. Serve warm.

Per Serving :

Calories: 542kcal / Carbs: 62g / Protein: 23g / Fat: 23g / Sodium: 1349mg

Zucchini Double Cheese Pizza

Prep Time : 4 mins / Cook: 9 mins / Servings: 2

Ingredients

- ½ Medium Zucchini courgette
- 3 Tbsp Soft Cheese
- 4 Slices Hard Cheese
- 2 Tsp Oregano
- Salt & Pepper

Preparation Instructions

1. Sprinkle salt and pepper over the nine slices of zucchini that are 1 cm thick.
2. Sprinkle salt and pepper over the nine slices of zucchini that are 1 cm thick.
3. On your grill pan, in the Ninja Foodi air fryer, for six minutes at 160 c/320 f.
4. Round up the cheese and set it away.
5. When the air fryer beeps, add a layer of soft cheese to each, press a cheese circle
6. Apply this to each of the nine slices of zucchini.
7. Cook for a further 3 minutes at 200 °C (400 °F).

Per Serving :

Calories: 311kcal / Carbs: 3g / Protein: 15g / Fat: 26g / Sodium: 421mg

Crispy air fryer potato salad

Prep time : 10 mins / Cook time: 25 min / Serves 4

Ingredients

- 2 tbsp olive oil
- 40g pkt French onion soup mix
- 4 streaky bacon rashers
- 1 tbsp fresh lemon juice
- 185g whole egg mayonnaise
- 1kg baby coliban potatoes, halved
- 125g sour cream
- ½ bunch chopped fresh chives

Preparation Instructions :

1. Oil, 60g mayonnaise, and soup mix should all be combined in a bowl. Potato has to be paired with. Place into the ninja foodi air fryer's basket. Air frying takes 15 minutes @ 200C. Shake the basket while hurling the potatoes. Add some bacon rashers to the potatoes. Continue air frying at 160C for an additional 10 minutes.
2. Combine the remaining mayonnaise, sour cream, chives, and lemon juice in a jug. Add pepper as a seasoning. To serve, place the potatoes in a plate. Top with the sour cream mixture. Make coarse bacon chops. To serve, scatter the potatoes on top.

Per Serving :

Calories: 3410 / fat: 61.9g / protein: 9.5g / carbs: 57.1g / Sodium: 1.9g

Air fryer vegetarian Christmas log

Prep time : 20 mins / Cook time: 20 min / Serves 6

Ingredients

- 1 tbsp olive oil
- 3 garlic cloves, crushed
- 500g frozen spinach, thawed, excess liquid squeezed
- 300g fresh ricotta, crumbled
- 1 tbsp finely grated lemon rind
- 2 ½ sheets frozen puff pastry, just thawed
- 1 brown onion, finely chopped
- 2 tsp fresh thyme leaves
- 180g haloumi, coarsely grated
- 2 eggs, plus 1 egg, lightly whisked
- Spicy tomato chutney, to serve

Preparation Instructions :

1. Over a medium-low flame, warm the oil in a frying pan. The onion should soften after 5 minutes of tossing and cooking. Add the thyme, onion, and garlic. Put in a large bowl.
2. The spinach, ricotta, haloumi, lemon peel, and 2 eggs are added to the onion mixture. Mix

thoroughly before combining. Season.

3. Place one entire sheet of pastry on a clean work surface. Place half of the spinach mixture on the dough, about three centimeters from the edge that is closest to you. Make a log out of the spinach mixture. Rolling up the pastry encloses the filling. Seal. Repeat with the remaining whole pastry sheet and spinach filling.

4. Rolls' tops should be delicately brushed with beaten egg. The leftover pastry may be cut into six 6 cm and six 3 cm stars using cookie cutters. stars on the logs' tops. Use egg to brush.

5. Preheat Ninja foodi air fryer at 180C for 3 minutes. Place rolls into the air fryer basket (see note). Cook for 20 minutes or until pastry is golden and filling is heated through. Slice and serve with chutney .

Per Serving :

Calories: 609cal / fat: 38.2g / protein: 22.1g / carbs: 47.3g / Sodium: 1.1g

Air fryer brie

Prep time : 5 mins / Cook time: 10 min / Serves 4

Ingredients

- 300g Castello Double Cream Brie
- 125g soft & juicy dried figs, quartered
- 1 sourdough baguette, sliced

- 125ml honey
- 1 fresh rosemary sprig, leaves picked
- Olive oil, to serve

Preparation Instructions :

1. Place a small saucepan over medium-high heat and add the honey, figs, and rosemary. Percolate for a time. Heat should be adjusted to low and simmer for a few minutes, or until figs are ready. Eliminate the heat. Set aside and let cool completely.

2. In the ninja foodi air fryer basket, put the baguette. Add a few drops of oil. Use salt to season. For five minutes or until golden, air fry at 180 °C.

3. Place brie in a small ovenproof dish or ramekin. Place in the air fryer basket. Air fry at 180°C for 6 minutes or until soft and gooey.

4. Over the brie, drizzle the honey mixture. Serve with slices of bread for dipping.

Per Serving :

Calories: 738 / fat: 31.1g / protein: 18.0g / carbs: 98.6g / Sodium: 889.3mg

Air Fryer Rotisserie Chicken

Prep time : 5 mins / Cook time: 50 mins / Serves 4

Ingredients

- 1 Medium Whole Chicken

- 1 Tbsp Extra Virgin Olive Oil
- 1 Tbsp Thyme
- 1 Tbsp Mixed Herbs
- Salt & Pepper

Preparation Instructions :

1. Tie the legs of your chicken up with string to hold them in position.
2. Grab your rod, put it through the chicken's neck, and then draw it out the other end at the chicken's bottom. The end clamps are then put into place.
3. Then, properly season the chicken before smearing it in extra virgin olive oil or your chosen substitute oil.
4. Make sure the whole chicken is stable and won't fall during rotisserie cooking before placing it in the air fryer oven.
5. At 180°C/360°F, air fried for 50 minutes. However, keep an eye on it for the first few of minutes to make sure it rotates correctly and remains in position. After that, take out of the air fryer and let stand for 5 minutes.

Per Serving :

Calories: 456kcal / Carbs: 1g / Protein: 36g / Fat: 33g / Sodium: 134mg

Air Fryer Ham

Prep time : 5 mins / Cook time: 50 mins / Serves 4

Ingredients

- 1.2 Kg Ham/Gammon Joint
- 6 Tbsp Honey
- 4 Tbsp Heinz Mustard
- 2 Tbsp Garlic Puree

Preparation Instructions :

1. Trim the ham's fat using a sharp knife. Score the ham joint in the shape of cubes.
2. After thoroughly mixing the honey, garlic, and mustard in a bowl, spread a thick coating of the marinade over the ham, making sure to get it into the scored areas.
3. Then, use your Ninja foodi air fryer to cook the ham that has been skewered on rods. After 25 minutes of cooking at 200°C/400°F, cook for a further 25 minutes at 170°C/340°F.
4. Once the rod has been removed, slice your ham.

Per Serving :

Calories: 845.98kcal / Carbs: 29.23g / Protein: 65.94g / Fat: 50.95g / Sodium: 3733.79mg

Chicken & Stuffing

Prep time : 8 mins / Cook time: 54 mins / Serves 4

Ingredients

- Small Whole Chicken
- 2 Tbsp Breadcrumbs heaped
- 1 Tsp Parsley
- 2 Tbsp Extra Virgin Olive Oil
- 2 Tsp Oregano
- 250 g Sausage Meat

- 2 Slices Stale Bread
- 1 Tbsp Sage
- 1 Tsp Thyme
- 1 Tsp Extra Virgin Olive Oil
- 1 Spring Onion sliced
- Salt & Pepper

Preparation Instructions :

1. Slice up pieces of crusty bread into croutons, add a teaspoon of extra virgin olive oil, and top with thyme. At 180°C/360°F, air fried for 4 minutes.
2. Add the remaining filling Ingredients to a bowl while the air fryer is cooking the croutons. Included in this are the spring onion slices, sausage, breadcrumbs, salt, pepper, sage, and parsley.
3. Add in the croutons and mix with your hands to make a huge stuffing ball.
4. Hold the chicken up and place the stuffing into the cavity, any leftover stuffing can then be reserved for stuffing balls.
5. Place the entire chicken on your clean cutting board, breast side up. Use some string to tie the legs. Add a tablespoon of extra virgin olive oil, along with salt, pepper, and oregano, to the blender. Put the chicken in the air fryer basket with the breasts facing up. Make sure no stuffing escapes by being cautious. 30 minutes of air frying at 170°C/340°F.
6. When the air fryer beeps, flip the food over and cook for a further 20 minutes on the other side at the same temperature, being sure to season and coat the other side.
7. After it beeps, let it rest for a few minutes before serving.

Per Serving :

Calories: 323kcal / Carbs: 12g / Protein: 12g / Fat: 25g / Sodium: 538mg

White Chocolate Chip Cookies

Prep time : 8 mins / Cook time: 8 mins / Serves 4

Ingredients

- 260 g Self Raising Flour
- 150 g Butter
- 3 Tbsp Whole Milk

- 120 g White Sugar
- 4 Tbsp Golden Syrup
- 1 Tsp Vanilla Essence

- 100 g Crushed White Chocolate
- 25 g White Chocolate Chips
- Handful White Chocolate Chips for on top

Preparation Instructions :

1. Butter and sugar should be combined in a bowl and then blended with a hand mixer to get a creamy consistency.
2. With the exception of the flour and white chocolate, add the remaining Ingredients and beat everything together with a hand mixer until it is smooth and creamy.
3. Use your hand mixer on the low setting to combine the flour with the other ingredients.
4. Then, add the Nestle white chocolate chips and the crushed pieces, and stir everything with a fork until it resembles cookie dough.
5. Make 4 equal pieces if you want huge cookies, or 8–12 if you want smaller ones. Then, form the mixture into cookies and place it onto a bed of foil for air-frying. At 180°C/360°F, air fry for 8 minutes.
6. Before serving, scatter a few additional white chocolate chips on top.

Per Serving :

Calories: 868kcal / Carbs: 114g / Protein: 10g / Fat: 42g / Sodium: 302mg

Cob loaf dip

Prep time : 35 mins / Cook time: 30 mins / Serves 8

Ingredients

- 450g cob loaf
- 3 garlic cloves, crushed
- 250g cream cheese, at room temperature, chopped
- 200g sour cream
- 125ml pure cream
- 250g frozen spinach, thawed
- 1 tbsp olive oil
- 1 brown onion, finely chopped
- 75g shredded 3 cheese mix
- 35g sachet salt-reduced French onion soup mix
- 3 green shallots, thinly sliced

Preparation Instructions :

1. Trim the top of the cob bread by 4 cm. The bread should now have a 1.5 cm thick shell in the center. Slice or roughly chop the top and inside of the loaf of bread. The ninja foodi air fryer should be filled with corn and bread bits. liberally with oil. Cook the basket for 8 minutes at 160°C, shaking it halfway through. the serving bowl upon transfer.
2. In the meanwhile, squeeze the excess liquid from the spinach using your hands.
3. Heat the oil in a large frying pan over medium-high heat. Cook onion and garlic for 5 minutes, or until softened, stirring often. Low-heat setting. Cream cheese, sour cream, pure cream, shredded cheese, and soup mix should all be added. Stir well to mix. Get rid of the heat. Add two-thirds of the shallot by stirring. Use pepper to season.

4. Spoon spinach mixture into loaf. Completely cover with foil. Place the loaf in air fryer. Cook at 160C for 15 minutes. Remove and discard foil. Cook for a further 5 minutes or until bread is toasted and dip is hot.
5. Sprinkle cob loaf with remaining onion and serve with toasted bread pieces.

Per Serving :

Calories: 450 cal / Carbs: 41.8g / Protein: 12.9g / Fat: 26.4g / Sodium: 739.8mg

Pork belly with Christmas glaze

Prep time : 10 mins / Cook time: 55 mins / Serves 4

Ingredients

- 1 tbsp sea salt
- 4-6 small pink lady apples
- Christmas glaze
- 60ml apple cider vinegar
- 2 tsp wholegrain mustard
- 40g butter, chilled, chopped
- 1kg piece pork belly, rind dried
- Steamed green beans, to serve, optional
- 125ml maple syrup
- 55g caster sugar
- ½ tsp mixed spice

Preparation Instructions :

1. Heat the ninja foodi air fryer at 200C for three minutes. Pork rind should be salted.   In the ninja foodi air fryer basket, mist oil. Put the meat in the prepared basket. Don't forget to grease the meat. After 25 minutes in the air fryer, the pork should start to crackle. There is a temperature drop of 160C. Apples should be added to the air fryer basket. The pork has to air fried for a further 30 minutes to finish cooking and become tender.
2. In the meanwhile, make the glaze. The maple syrup, vinegar, sugar, mustard, and mixed spices should all be placed in a small pot over medium heat. boiling point. Over low heat, simmer the glaze for 5 minutes, or until it is thick and syrupy. Add the cold butter and stir.
3. Place sliced pork on a serving platter. If using, serve with steaming green beans and apples. To serve, drizzle the glaze over top.

Per Serving :

Calories: 1587cal / Carbs: 55.0g / Protein: 23g / Fat: 140.4g / Sodium: 929.3mg

Burrata bomb

Prep time : 10 mins / Cook time: 12 mins / Serves 4

Ingredients

- 250g store-bought fresh pizza dough

- Flour, for dusting
- 75g sun-dried tomato pesto
- 1/4 cup fresh basil leaves
- 150g burrata
- 60g salted butter, melted
- Thick balsamic vinegar, to serve (optional)
- Green salad, to serve (optional)

Preparation Instructions :

1. Spread the pesto over the dough, leaving a 6 to 8 cm border all around, and then roll out to a circle 30 cm in diameter on a floured surface. Top the pesto with basil leaves and a burrata ball in the center. The uncovered pastry should be covered with melted butter. Fold the dough over the burrata to create a package, and then roll it over the folds to seal.
2. Add melted butter to the basket of the Ninja Foodi air fryer before adding the food. The dough should be air-fried at 170°C for 10 to 12 minutes, or until golden and cooked through.
3. Serve with a drizzle of balsamic vinegar and a salad , if desired.

Per Serving :

Calories: 424cal / Carbs: 34.2g / Protein: 9.7g / Fat: 28.1g / Sodium: 639.3mg

French onion tarts

Prep time : 10 mins / Cook time: 30 mins / Serves 2

Ingredients

- 2 sheets shortcrust pastry, just thawed
- 2 tbsp sour cream
- 3 large eggs
- 1 small brown onion, thinly sliced
- Chopped fresh chives, to serve (optional)
- 75g cream cheese
- 25g grated cheddar
- 1 tbsp olive oil

Preparation Instructions :

1. Grease two 11.5 cm fluted tartlet pans lightly.
2. Place one pastry sheet on a work surface that has been lightly coated with flour. On top, add the last pastry layer. Roll out the dough with a little flour added until it is 3 mm thick. Cut in half diagonally. Gently insert one half in the prepared tart pan. Repeat with the second tart pan and second piece of dough. Remove any excess pastry. After lining the pastry casings with parchment paper, fill them with rice or pastry weights. Food should be placed in the air fryer basket and cooked for 6 minutes at 200C. Remove the paper and air fried the rice or beans for a further two minutes.
3. Meanwhile, heat the oil in a frying pan over medium heat. Add onion and cook, stirring occasionally, for 10 minutes or until golden and caramelised. Set aside to cool slightly.

4. Combine cream cheese , sour cream , cheddar and 1 egg in a bowl. Add the onion. Stir to combine. Season. Divide the mixture between tart cases. Make a small well in the centre of 1 tart. Crack an egg into the well. Repeat with remaining tart and egg. Season with pepper.

5. Air fry at 170C for 10-12 minutes or until just cooked. Leave in the air fryer to cool for 5 minutes or until the egg is cooked to your liking. Sprinkle with chives , if using, to serve.

Per Serving :

Calories: 2166cal) / Carbs: 166.5g / Protein: 39.3g / Fat: 149.0g / Sodium: 824.2mg

Ratatouille & Persian feta filo parcels

Prep time : 30 mins / Cook time: 1 hr / Serves 4

Ingredients

- 2 tbsp olive oil
- 32g chopped fresh continental parsley
- 12 sheets filo pastry
- 100g Persian feta, crumbled
- 2 large zucchini, cut into 1cm pieces
- 1 large eggplant, cut into 1cm pieces
- Basil pesto, to serve

- 2 tsp plain flour
- 2 tbsp sherry vinegar or red wine vinegar
- 100g butter, melted, cooled
- 2 green shallots, thinly sliced
- 1 red capsicum, deseeded, cut into 1cm pieces
- 1 garlic clove, finely chopped
- Rocket, to serve

Preparation Instructions :

1. Set the oven to 220°C or 200°C with the fan on. The shallot should be put in a big bowl. Add the oil, garlic, eggplant, and zucchini. Combine by seasoning and tossing. Place on a baking sheet, then bake for 15 minutes. Until the veggies are soft and light golden, stir and bake for a further 5 minutes.

2. Vegetables with flour on top should be combined by stirring. Add parsley and vinegar and stir. Set alone for cooling.

3. Bake at 180°/160° fan forced. Use baking paper to line a baking pan. Brush a sheet of filo pastry with with butter before placing it on a spotless work surface. Add 2 more filo sheets, a bit more butter, and another layer. Divide the stack in half across. Apply some butter on the brush. Fill the center with a quarter of the ratatouille. In the mixture, make a tiny well. Fill the well with one-fourth of the feta. Bring the pastry's edges toward the center while gently scrunching it to partly surround the filling. Make three additional packages by repeating.

4. Transfer parcels to prepared tray. Bake for 35-40 minutes or until golden. Cool slightly. Drizzle with pesto and serve with rocket .

Per Serving :

Calories: 610cal / Carbs: 34g / Protein: 15g / Fat: 44g

Chocolate Profiteroles

Prep time : 15 mins / Cook time: 20 mins / Serves 9

Ingredients

- 100 g Butter
- 200 g Plain Flour
- 6 Medium Eggs
- 300 ml Water
- Cream Filling:
- 2 Tsp Vanilla Essence
- 2 Tsp Icing Sugar
- 300 ml Whipped Cream
- Chocolate Sauce:
- 100 g Milk Chocolate broken into chunks
- 2 Tbsp Whipped Cream
- 50 g Butter

Preparation Instructions :

1. Preheat the airfryer to 170c.
2. In a large pan, combine the lard and water. Cook over medium heat, making sure to bring the mixture to a boil.
3. When it forms a large dough in the center of the pan, turn the heat back on after removing it from the heat and stirring in the flour (a little at a time).
4. Set aside the dough so it can cool. Add the eggs and fully incorporate once the mixture has been properly blended.
5. Make into profiterole shapes and bake at 180 degrees for 10 minutes.
6. Whipping cream, vanilla extract, and icing sugar are combined to make a wonderful, thick cream filling while the eclairs are baking.
7. The chocolate topping is prepared by mixing the chocolate, butter, and cream in a glass bowl and placing it over a pan of boiling water while the profiteroles are baking. Blend thoroughly until chocolate has melted.
8. Put melted chocolate on top of your profiteroles to complete them.

Per Serving :

Calories: 390kcal / Carbs: 28g / Protein: 7g / Fat: 27g / Sodium: 167mg

Fat Rascals

Prep time : 10 mins / Cook time: 11 mins / Serves 4

Ingredients

- 120 g Self Raising Flour
- 120 g Plain Flour
- 60 g Mixed Peel
- 1 Medium Orange zest only
- 1 Medium Lemon zest only
- 1 Tbsp Vanilla Essence
- 1 Tsp Cinnamon
- 1 Tsp Mixed Spice
- 100 g Unsalted Butter
- 40 g Caster Sugar
- 60 g Currants
- Pinch Nutmeg
- 1 Small Egg beaten
- 2 Tbsp Skimmed Milk
- Glace Cherries for decoration

Preparation Instructions :

1. Add the pieces of butter to the bowl with the flour, flavors, and sugar.
2. To make coarse, brown breadcrumbs, mix the lard, sugar, salt, and flour in a bowl.
3. The currants, peel, and zest are then added, along with the vanilla essence.
4. Once the dough is pliable enough to resemble a scone, add just enough milk to finish the recipe.
5. After that, measure out your mixture and divide it by 4. Then measure out the dough and divide it into 4 balls of equal size. After that, form into scones.
6. Decorate the tops with raisins for the grin, mixed peel for the nose, and glace cherry halves for the eyes.
7. Using a pastry brush, apply egg wash on the rascals' tops.
8. Fill the air fryer with the ingredients, and air fry for 8 minutes at 180°C/360°F, then 3 minutes at 160°C/320°F.

Per Serving :

Calories: 581kcal / Carbs: 87g / Protein: 10g / Fat: 22g / Sodium: 45mg

Air Fryer Rock Cakes

Prep time : 10 mins / Cook time: 8 mins / Serves 7

Ingredients

- 100 g Currants
- 225 g Self Raising Flour
- 100 g Unsalted Butter
- 30 g Mixed Peel

- 50 g Caster Sugar
- 1 Medium Egg
- 60 ml Skimmed Milk

Preparation Instructions :

1. The flour and sugar should be combined in a bowl before adding the cubed butter.
2. When you've combined the flour, sugar, and lard, you should have a bowl of coarse breadcrumbs.
3. The egg, currants, and peel should then be properly combined.
4. Then add just enough milk to create a sticky dough. adding a small amount of milk at a time until the dough resembles an excessively sticky scone batter or an extremely thick cake batter.
5. As you pour the mixture into the air fryer, line it with foil since the rock buns will be sticky.
6. Then, using a tablespoon, divide the batter over the foil to make room for four blobs of rock cake batter in the air fryer basket.
7. The food was then air-fried for 8 minutes at 180°C/360°F, if necessary in batches. then spread jam and butter on top.

Per Serving :

Calories: 313kcal / Carbs: 45g / Protein: 6g / Fat: 13g / Sodium: 25mg

Air Fryer Pumpkin Pie

Prep time : 10 mins / Cook time: 19 mins / Serves 8

Ingredients

- 500 g Pie Crust
- 500 g Instant Pot Pumpkin Pie Filling

Preparation Instructions :

1. Make your pumpkin pie filling first, then proceed. Always do this first so that I can prepare the pie crust while the pressure cooks. Approximately 500g of cubed pumpkin is all that is needed to make a medium-sized pie.
2. While it is under pressure, prepare your pie crust. After mixing the lard into the flour, sugar, and mixture, add the water gradually until the dough is pliable enough to form a pie crust.
3. To make your cake pan non-stick, spray it with extra virgin olive oil and massage it in with your hands.
4. After that, cover the cake pan with the pumpkin pie dough you just rolled out on a clean work surface dusted with flour. Edges should be cut. Mix your pumpkin pie filling and then pour it over your pie crust when the instant pot beeps.
5. Place the raw pumpkin pie in the air fryer, then cook it for an additional 5 minutes at 160°C (340°F) after 12 minutes at 170°C (340°F).
6. If you have extra pie dough and filling, roll part of it out and cut it into small pies.
7. Then load into the air fryer and cook for 12 minutes at 170c/340f.

Per Serving :

Calories: 351kcal / Carbs: 47g / Protein: 5g / Fat: 16g / Sodium: 386mg

Cheese Flan

Prep time : 10 mins / Cook time: 17 mins / Serves 8

Ingredients

- Pie Crust
- 4 Large Eggs
- 180 g Grated Cheese
- Salt & Pepper
- ½ Small Onion diced
- 120 ml Semi Skimmed Milk
- 2 Tsp Parsley

Preparation Instructions :

1. Prepared, rolled out, and placed to the tart pan should be shortcrust pastry.
2. Fork the bottom of the pastry to let it breathe.
3. Onion slices should then be added to the flan's base.
4. Combine the milk, eggs, and spices using a fork. Once the cheese has been added, thoroughly mix.
5. After covering the onions with the cheese and egg mixture, put the cheese flan in the air fryer.
6. 17 minutes at 160 c/320 f or until a cocktail stick inserted into the cheese flan comes out clean. After that, cut the flan into squares like a school lunch.

Per Serving :

Calories: 136kcal / Carbs: 4g / Protein: 10g / Fat: 9g / Sodium: 432mg

Air Fryer Cupcakes

Prep time : 20 mins / Cook time: 12 mins / Serves 10

Ingredients

- 200 g Buttercream
- 120 g Caster Sugar
- 1 Tbsp Vanilla Paste
- Food Colouring optional
- 120 g Unsalted Butter
- 120 g Self Raising Flour
- 2 Large Eggs

Preparation Instructions :

1. In a stand mixer, combine the butter and sugar. Mix the Ingredients for three minutes.
2. Clean the sides, then blend the eggs, vanilla, and speed 3 for an additional three minutes.
3. Following that, add the flour and mix on speed 4 for a minute. Next, scrape the edges.
4. Cupcake batter should be poured into tiny pudding dishes after reaching the quarter-full point in paper liners.

5. For 12 minutes, cook the meal in the air fryer at 160 °C (320 °F). Give a cooling tray time to cool entirely.
6. Make your buttercream first, then clean the mixer If you want rainbow cupcakes, load the Ingredients into different dishes with food coloring.
7. After the cupcakes have cooled, place the piping bag over the glass and insert the nozzle. Use your hands to firmly twist the piping bag after adding the buttercream, then affix a peg to the top. The piping bag's bottom should be cut off so that the nozzle may pass through.
8. Pipe your cupcakes and then serve.

Per Serving :
Calories: 262kcal / Carbs: 22g / Protein: 3g / Fat: 18g / Sodium: 20mg

S'mores

Prep time : 2 mins / Cook time: 6 mins / Serves 10

Ingredients
- 8 Graham Crackers
- 4 Marshmallows
- 8 Squares Galaxy Chocolate

Preparation Instructions :
1. As you assemble your ingredients, make sure that each air-fried smore has 2 squares of chocolate and a marshmallow. Make sure the chocolate is also at room temperature.
2. Cut the marshmallows in half width-wise rather than length-wise to make them sticky.
3. The crackers and the sticky half of the two marshmallows should then be placed in the ninja foodi air fryer basket.
4. Like when it is grilled, the marshmallow should be air-fried for 6 minutes at 180°C/360°F or until the top turns brown.
5. Place the chocolate on top of each marshmallow half before it starts to cool, and then top with a cracker.
6. Once the marshmallow has been covered with melting chocolate, serve.

Per Serving :
Calories: 425kcal / Carbs: 61g / Protein: 4g / Fat: 22g / Sodium: 199mg

Bread And Butter Pudding

Prep time : 5 mins / Cook time: 10 mins / Serves 5

Ingredients
- 4 Slices Stale Thick Sliced Bread
- 1 Tsp Vanilla Essence

- 120 ml Semi Skimmed Milk
- 2 Tbsp Butter
- 240 ml Double Cream
- 1 Tsp Cinnamon
- Icing Sugar optional
- 240 ml Raisins
- 3 Large Eggs
- 80 ml Caster Sugar
- Extra Virgin Olive Oil Spray

Preparation Instructions :

1. Crack the eggs into a bowl, then add the cream, sugar, vanilla, and cinnamon. Blend with a fork.
2. Cut your bread into thick slices.
3. The bread should be completely coated in the batter once you've fully mixed the ingredients.
4. Your air fryer will be prepared by being drizzled with extra virgin olive oil and then being sprinkled with a pastry brush.
5. Fill the air fryer with batter-soaked bread, leaving any little pieces that would break up inside, and cook for 5 minutes at 190°C/380°F.
6. Place the bread in the bowl with the little pieces, then stir in the milk and raisins.
7. Put the bowl's contents in a container that is appropriate for air frying, and then sprinkle some butter on top. At 200c/400f, air fried for an additional 5 minutes. Before serving, add some icing sugar.

Per Serving :

Calories: 514kcal / Carbs: 67g / Protein: 9g / Fat: 26g / Sodium: 207mg

Carrot Cake

Prep time : 12 mins / Cook time: 41 mins / Serves 12

Ingredients

- 225 g Self Raising Flour
- 1 Tsp Mixed Spice
- 1 Tsp Ground Ginger
- 150 ml Extra Virgin Olive Oil
- 30 g Caster Sugar/Granulated Sugar
- 2 Large Eggs
- 85 g Philadelphia Cream Cheese
- 60 g Icing Sugar
- 2 Tbsp Semi Skimmed Milk
- 1 Tsp Cinnamon
- ¼ Tsp Nutmeg
- 150 g Brown Sugar
- 2 Large Carrots
- Carrot Cake Frosting
- 16 g Butter
- 1 Tsp Vanilla Essence

Preparation Instructions :

1. After the carrots have been peeled, grind them using a grater.
2. The flour, grated carrot, sugars, and all the seasonings should be mixed together in a bowl with a fork. Make a well in the center, then put your cracked eggs inside. Use a hand mixer to completely blend after adding the oil.

3. As you gradually add the milk, watch that the batter for the carrots is not too thick.

4. After putting the carrot cake batter to the silicone, place it in the ninja foodi air fryer basket. After 26 minutes of frying at 170°C (340°F) and 15 minutes at 180°C (360°F) in the air fryer, a cocktail stick should come out clean.

5. Allow to cool and then whilst it is cooling make your cream cheese frosting. Start by adding the icing sugar and the butter into a bowl and mixing with your hand mixer. Then add in the other Ingredients and then mix again.

6. After the cake has cooled, level it out by chopping off the top with a bread knife.

7. The icing is then spooned on. To evenly distribute the frosting over the carrot cake's top, use the back of a spoon.

8. Slice into 8 equal sections after cooling fully in the refrigerator for one hour.

Per Serving :

Calories: 307kcal / Carbs: 35g / Protein: 4g / Fat: 17g / Sodium: 55mg

Air Fryer Chocolate Chip Cookies

Prep time : 8 mins / Cook time: 8 mins / Serves 4

Ingredients

- 260 g Self Raising Flour
- 3 Tbsp Whole Milk
- 100 g Milk Chocolate Chunks
- 80 g Brown Sugar
- 150 g Butter
- 4 Tbsp Golden Syrup
- 1 Tsp Vanilla Essence
- 25 g Chocolate Chips
- 40 g White Sugar
- Handful Chocolate Chips for on top

Preparation Instructions :

1. Put the butter and sugars in a bowl, and then combine the fat and sugar with a hand mixer to create a creamy consistency.

2. With the exception of the flour and chocolate, blend everything else with a hand mixer until the mixture is smooth and creamy.

3. Use your hand mixer on the low setting to combine the flour with the other ingredients.

4. The mixture will now resemble cookie dough; add your chocolate and combine with a fork after that.

5. Create 8–12 smaller cookies or 4 equal-sized large cookies. After that, form into cookies and place on a foil bed before loading into the air fryer. 8 minutes of air frying at

6. Add some extra chocolate chips on top before serving.

Per Serving :

Calories: 874kcal / Carbs: 112g / Protein: 10g / Fat: 43g / Sodium: 286mg

Air Fryer Chocolate Chip Cookies

Prep time : 10 mins / Cook time: 8 mins / Serves 6

Ingredients

- 250 g Self Raising Flour
- 175 g Butter
- 75 g Sugar

Preparation Instructions :

1. In a bowl, combine the butter, sugar, and flour. Use a knife to quickly prepare the butter by cutting it into little pieces.
2. With your hands, incorporate the fat into the flour and sugar until it resembles breadcrumbs. After that, combine everything and include a tiny amount of shortbread dough.
3. On a kitchen counter that has been dusted with flour, roll out your shortbread.
4. When preparing festive shortbread or classic shortbread cookies, use rounds and cut into the required shapes.
5. Add a layer of foil into the air fryer basket and then place the shortbread over it.
6. Air fry for 8 minutes at 180c/360f then allow to cool.

Per Serving :

Calories: 408kcal / Carbs: 43g / Protein: 5g / Fat: 24g / Sodium: 209mg

Air Fryer Banana Souffle

Prep time : 3 mins / Cook time: 15 mins / Serves 4

Ingredients

- 2 Medium Bananas
- ½ Tsp Cinnamon
- 2 Large Eggs
- Extra Virgin Olive Oil Spray

Preparation Instructions :

1. Crack the eggs into the blender along with the peeled bananas. On the pulse setting, add your cinnamon and mix until smooth.
2. Spray your ramekins with extra virgin olive oil.
3. Pour the souffle batter into the ramekins, then place them in the air fryer basket.
4. 15 minutes of air frying at 180 C/360 F.
5. Serve immediately before the souffles start to collapse.

Per Serving :

Calories: 85kcal / Carbs: 14g / Protein: 3g / Fat: 2g / Sodium: 32mg

Printed in Great Britain
by Amazon